THOMAS MERTON

MEDITATIONS ON LITURGY

MOWBRAYS
LONDON & OXFORD

Acknowledgment is made to the editors of *Commonweal*, *The Critic*, and *Worship*, in whose pages some of these articles first appeared in somewhat different form.

Originally published 1965 under the title *Seasons of Celebration* in the United States of America.

First published in Great Britain 1976 by
A. R. Mowbray & Company Limited
The Alden Press, Osney Mead, Oxford OX2 0EG

Printed in Great Britain by
Redwood Burn Limited
Trowbridge & Esher

ISBN: 0 264 66353 5 paper
      0 264 66363 2 cased

Contents

‧§ iii

INTRODUCTION

It is more than ten years since the essays contained in this book were collected and published in America but it is entirely appropriate that they should be made available in England at this moment. Liturgy has undergone drastic changes in the last twenty years and most of these were under way when Thomas Merton wrote these essays. His comments in the first two chapters on liturgical change seem prophetic in their application to the state of liturgy today.

The great value of the liturgical renewal of this century has not lain primarily in its astringent return to the patterns of the early church but in its concern to find through those patterns a way to focus the whole life of a living and contemporary community on Christ as a worshipping assembly. This has meant a period of continual change and experiment in external ritual, the re-evaluation of symbols and the use of modern language. It is a process that has proved invigorating but it is without question that it carries within itself serious dangers to that which it is primarily concerned to express. Liturgy is not a performance; it is prayer and it is prayer which is ritual, a 'ritus', a series of recurring events. It is not the everchanging presentation of our present interests and understanding but a way into mysteries beyond our apprehension, and which are reached not by the mind alone but by the participation of the whole of man living within the community of faith, on earth and in heaven. If forms of worship monopolise attention for too long, the strain can become too great and a malaise sets in, self-consciousness about externals deflects us from the central mystery of worship in a way that is quickly destructive to our life in Christ.

It is into a situation which bears many signs of this danger that Fr Merton's essays come like water in a dry land. Writing as a monk of a contemplative order and as a man fully alive to his times, he is able to combine, as in so much of his writing, the deep insight of the man of prayer with a keen and vigorous appreciation of liturgy as renewed today. In these essays he considers the major liturgical themes from Advent to Easter so that their eternal meaning and relevance is made clear. It is a book that belongs to the monastic life which experiences liturgy as the pivot of daily life wherein the community continually realises the mysteries of the Kingdom as 'God in Christ reconciling the world to Himself'. It is the essential function of the monk to live the liturgy in this way; when a monk is also able to communicate this interior heart of the liturgy to his contemporaries, as Fr Merton does here, he offers a way in which new and unfamiliar liturgical forms can become again 'wells of living water, springing up into eternal life' (John 4, 14).

BASIL HUME
Archbishop of Westminster

I

LITURGICAL RENEWAL:
THE OPEN APPROACH

What is meant by liturgical renewal, and what are some of the problems involved? We, the ordinary clergy and laity, the commoners in the "people of God" need to understand this well, because the main job of renewal is ours. Liturgical reform merely from the top down, renewal by juridical *fiat* alone, is not really likely to work. Yet this is apparently the way many are expecting it to "happen."

Those who are passionately dedicated to the liturgical movement may perhaps be attaching too much importance to the fact that certain desirable changes, have been, will be, or at any rate always *can* be legislated. But, as we are aware from the civil rights, conflict, the mere opening of new ways by law does not mean that one can always travel them in fact. Hence those those who are not so enthusiastic about liturgical renewal are perhaps consoling themselves with stoical reflections on the unwillingness and incapacity of most priests and laypeople to make the required changes in such a way as to effect a real and basic renewal of worship.

Changes are certainly being made. There can be no question that now, after nearly a year of the "new

Mass," the changes are pointing in the right direction. Obviously the reform has only begun. The "new Mass," as it now stands, seems to represent certain practical compromises that were needed in order that a certain amount of vernacular might be allowed. But it certainly does seem illogical to switch from English to Latin just for the Prayer and then go back to English for the Epistle; or to say "The Lord be with you" now in English and now in Latin. The logic of Liturgical renewal certainly requires that the entire Mass be said in the language of the people, and this must eventually come. At the same time we may remark in passing that the old Roman, Ambrosian and other liturgies in Latin can and should be preserved in some monasteries that might be willing to dedicate themselves to this work (Solesmes, for example).

The best thing about the "new Mass" is the real opening up of opportunities for participation. With the altar now facing the people, there is obviously more sense of communication on both sides, and much less danger of the old wool-gathering distractedness which always threatens the man who is merely absorbed in his own routine thoughts and imaginings. Communication being consciously established and maintained, priest and people can more easily become aware that they are together *celebrating* the mystery of our Redemption in the Eucharistic Sacrifice and the Lord's Supper.

The presence of a lay-commentator telling people when to stand, sit, and so on, and offering capsule explanations of what is going on, is of course a temporary expedient. It is not to be regarded as an un-mixed blessing and the sooner everyone is able to get along without it, the better. But of course it is most desirable that a layman should participate by reading the Epistle, for example.

Concelebration and Communion under both spe-cies have been among the most impressive and praiseworthy additions to the new Liturgy, but con-celebration is still of necessity confined mostly to monastic communities.

Obviously all is not yet perfect. Those who imag-ined that it was enough to have the texts trans-lated into the vernacular were perhaps unprepared for the problems that might still remain. Our Bible readings are now in English. But what English! A text is being used that was prepared for private reading and study, and its attempts at bright col-loquialism do not stand up well under the exig-encies of public and solemn celebration. A certain sacred and timeless seriousness is required in our vernacular liturgical texts, or they will rapidly be-come unbearably trite.

Complaints are made about the hymn singing, and doubtless it is not always up to 'the standard of Gregorian. But at least it is something that every-one can do. How many parishes were there, before the Council, where *all* the congregation knew how to sing the common of the Mass in Gregorian?

There remains very much to be done. We are in a period of transition. Neither misplaced enthusiasms nor resentful non-participation will help the Church now. We must go forward in a .spirit of sober and reasonable experimentation, and this means facing the hazards of trial and error. No matter what changes are made, if they are only new gestures performed in the old spirit, they will not constitute a liturgical renewal. It is not the old forms that must go so much as the old spirit. So let us take a quick look at the "old spirit," fully aware that it does not belong only to the past. It is still very much with us, even with some of those who favor progressive ideas!

Brevity always involves some risk of caricature, but obviously not much paper needs to be wasted on the familiar rigidities, the inarticulate, cramped, official and antiquated style of common worship before Vatican II. The defects are not so much in the style itself as in the psychological residue which years of this kind of worship have accumulated in the spirituality and the performance of priest and people. Incapacity to communicate together and indeed a general lack of desire to communicate all add up to a kind of consecrated bashfulness. Sacraments which imply a full, deep, open-hearted sharing in personal warmth and love, have actually become signs of a consecrated impersonality and of business-like despatch.

What difference does it make if the priest says the whole canon out loud if it still means something like this: "I am the priest, you are the laity, and this is a strictly business deal. You have your place and I have mine. I am here to confect valid sacraments for you to receive and you are there because if you were not there I would not be here confecting sacraments. Besides everyone knows that unless I exercise my special office as the only one who can validly make Our Lord sacramentally present, you won't even have a religion. Indeed you will be, for all intents, and purposes, godless. As to who you are or what you think about all this, I couldn't care less. So let's get the whole thing over with so that I can go mind my business and you yours."

This is the mentality which one of our best liturgists, Dom Adrien Nocent, has called "validism." According to this outlook, what matters is not that the ceremonies have meaning, or that the sacraments eloquently speak the grace which they signify, or that the order and comeliness of worship should help to manifest the splendor of God's love and of His presence in the midst of His people. All that matters is that the sacraments be valid, the formulas correct, and the gestures rubrically exact. Worship is mechanically efficient, the worshipper gets grace with a minimum of trouble, and all goes smoothly!

This mentality is responsible for a deadly atmosphere of officialism in cult, a pervasive and deadening influence which one is expected to counteract by interior and subjective worship, governed entirely by one's own individual tastes and needs and which, in the last analysis, is one's own responsibility and nobody else's business.

Let me say at once that this private realm of sincerity and personal awareness is not to be scoffed at. Where worship is cold, formal, official and empty of personal communication, what other refuge is left for the worshipper? I am not too sure I think it is a good thing to make him feel guilty about it, unless you have something better to offer here and now, in the concrete and not just on paper or in your own head.

What is required above all is a new spirit of _openness,_ in which the priest is open to his people, and they are open to him and one another. This means that the words of the liturgy should be spoken by a person, to persons, and not just uttered abstractly in a sacred void.

It is true, and this is sometimes forgotten, that the words of the Liturgy are sacred and the people are gathered in a "sacred space." "The Lord be with you" is something else again than "Hello gang!" So the whole idea of "renewal" means something else than saying the formulas of prayer in a familiar language and with the intonations of colloquial and rotarian togetherness. It means discovering a _new_ sense of sacred space, of community, of oneness in the Spirit, as a result of a communication on a deep level with which we have long ceased to be familiar: it means learning to experience the mystery of oneness in grace. This demands a community presence and awareness that is distinct from our ordinary assemblies: a presence to one another in Christ. A presence also in celebration. It means therefore a sense of mystery. One cannot possibly experience this liturgical presence and oneness if one is not open to the reality of the Spirit in and through all who have been brought together in the worshipping assembly. Yet this sense is not mystical and esoteric. It is based on our natural human affinities for one another as beings with the same needs, the same joys, the same hopes, fears and loves, who have been brought together by

the merciful love of Christ. The words, songs, ceremonies, signs, movements of worship are all designed,
by their very nature, to open the mind and heart of
the participant to this experience of oneness in
Christ. But this sacramental consciousness depends
first of all on human sympathy, relatedness and on
some degree of mutual understanding. Hence the
obligation to be at peace with all before going to
worship.

One reason why I am a Catholic, a monk and a
priest today is that I first went to Mass, and kept
going to Mass, in a Church where these things were
realized. No matter how progressive Father Ford may
have been (and, thank God, still is), Corpus Christi
Church had the same Roman liturgy as everyone else
in 1938. It was just the familiar Mass that is now
being radically reformed. There was nothing new or
revolutionary about it; only that everything was well
done, not out of aestheticism or rubrical obsessive-
ness, but out of love for God and His truth. It would
certainly be ingratitude of me if I did not remember
the atmosphere of joy, light, and at least relative
openness and spontaneity that filled Corpus Christi at
solemn High Mass.

One of the extraordinary things about Corpus
Christi Church is that it unashamedly goes back to a
rather dim period in worship and art. The sanctuary
has a seventeenth-century look. But it is the air of
Caroline Anglicanism as well as of Baroque Catholic-
ity. It has no baroque excess about it, but it is consciously splendid, in an honest, forthright way. I suppose the particular truthfulness of Corpus Christi is

that it is one of the few Catholic Churches in America that has had the courage to look "Colonial" and "Early American" without fear of being labelled "Protestant." There is enough about the tabernacle, candlesticks, and the ritual itself that is purely Roman, Post-Tridentine Roman. The paradox is then that here was a progressive who was able to get more out of all the things the conservatives claim to prize than the conservatives themselves!

So it is not the style that matters but the spirit, the taste, the living sense of rightness and of truth, and basically the respect for God's creation, God's people, God's house. Where these are found, there is also inevitably a natural and supernatural openness, because we are made in such a way that we respond to such order and such harmony by opening our hearts and lifting them up to the light.

I remember also the side altar in the Lady Chapel at Corpus Christi with its lovely primitive Italian tryptich, its painted wooden Mexican candlesticks, its rich antependium, all these things which will probably "have to go." It does not matter. Whatever may be the rite or the style, there is none that cannot be redeemed by a certain openness, innocence, awareness, light and trust. But to say this is not to exempt from reform those styles which tend by their nature to favor rigidity and therefore to close the heart and mind to a genuine and more open participation in the liturgical mystery.

But let us be quite clear what we are participating *in*. Is Christian worship to be communion in correctness or communion in love? Oneness in Law or oneness in Christ? Sharing in valid sacraments or in the Spirit of Life that is in the Risen Savior? Certainly we must be correct, we must intelligently obey the laws of the Church and we must be concerned with the validity of the sacraments: but we are mistaken if we end there. These things are not the whole of worship. They are not the end, they are only the beginning. If we see no further than the beginning, we may even fail to begin.

We must learn to participate in a free, open, joyous communion of love and praise. Whatever helps this sense of freedom, of openness, I would even say, of *unconstraint,* is going to help the liturgical renewal. Whatever continues to foster rigidity, suspiciousness, timidity, coldness and resentment is going to threaten the liturgical reform with sterility. The great enemy is *constraint,* which brings all these other devils with it.

Let us go back to the *Acts of the Apostles.* The first Christians were people who abounded in irrepressible joy and trust because they realized they were now free and *no longer had to worship under constraint.* Whatever may have been the real qualities of Jewish spirituality at the time, the Christians believed that the Torah required a rigid servitude to forms that had now become empty. The martyrs laid down their lives rather than suffer constraint and obey the official and juridical command to sacrifice to the Roman Emperor. Christian worship in its beginnings is marked by a general, explicit, uncompromising refusal of constraint.

Both progressives and conservatives seem to place

their trust in legislation to attain their ends. But liturgical renewal will not be made by laws, and it cannot be prevented by laws. There is danger in the widespread identification of *constraint* with *order.* Obviously, it will do no good simply to constrain progressives to be content with old forms that seem to them lifeless. Just as obviously, those who do not feel or understand the need for renewal cannot be brought into open and living participation merely by constraint.

The progressives do not rely on the force of law in the same way as the conservatives. But even on the progressive side one sometimes feels there is a tendency to exert psychological pressure. The attempt is humanly understandable and I for one do not resent it. But it is a possible source of constraint, and I think this needs to be noted, for it will work against renewal in the long run.

For instance, some rather forceful statements, no doubt substantially correct, have been made insinuating that conservative fears of change might well have a psychoneurotic foundation. Well and good. The fear, the hesitation, the bashfulness-to-the-point-of-panic that characterize some neurotics, and make all forms of communal and interpersonal relationships potentially agonizing to them, obviously do not dispose them to welcome new and strange situations in which they foresee that they will feel threatened. It is quite true that the risks of reform and change will be disturbing to the insecure. But let us remember that too great an eagerness to play on this insecurity and to "punish" the prospective non-participant in advance is not necessarily a sign of perfect psychic balance. There are all kinds of neurotics, and those who project their insecurity on others instead of feeling it themselves are not the ones who are in the best shape.

It is obvious that a situation like this which brings into play the forces of insecurity, of authority, of risk, of change, of law and so on, will naturally create all kinds of inner conflicts, some of which will be felt, others of which will be "acted out" perhaps in a very aggressive and authoritarian fashion by the very ones who are setting themselves up as champions of liberty and of renewal. The insecure will naturally tend to prefer a status quo guaranteed by law and familiar practice, because they depend on knowing what to expect. To point this out to them is no way of winning them over, and let us admit that if the aims of liturgical renewal are to be achieved, such people must be won over reasonably and gently, not bullied into complying.

On the contrary, when a person suffering from anxiety, insecurity and feelings of inferiority concludes that the liturgical movement regards him with suspicion and hostility because he is ill at ease with other people and would rather die than do something new and strange, he feels menaced. He is the object of a great, vague, nameless, limitless, unidentifiable threat. He does not know precisely how he is threatened. He does not know the reason for it. He does not know for sure just what will punish him and for what sin, still less what he can do to appease the hostile forces. All he knows is that because he is what he is (shy, scared, insecure) there are certain people (liturgists) who disapprove of him. They intend to show him up, and liturgy will be their occasion for doing it. He has protected himself and his shyness in worship by approaching God under a comforting anonymity, hitherto guaranteed by inviolable law. Now this trusted protection is going to be brutally and mercilessly removed. He is going to be left defenceless, without any means of understanding his plight or of handling it: and if he cannot handle it he will feel himself for all intents and purposes, excommunicated.

At the same time the aggressive type will be going through a different syndrome. He too is insecure, but he must at all costs prevent himself from seeing it and feeling it. He is the one who is never at a loss, always in the forefront, always a leader. Even if he does not really know what he is leading and where he is going, he has to be out in front. Just to make quite sure that no feeling of dissent become conscious, he overplays his role. And so, in the congregation of twelve at a dialogue Mass, he is the one who bellows out the responses, reducing everyone else to a state of tongue-tied embarrassment and spiritual paralysis. This of course comes to his attention. What does he do about it? He falls back on the absolute imperative: he has been asked to participate and he will participate even if it means the end of all spontaneous participation by anybody else and also by himself. He is an absolutist who acts under such constraint that he constrains everyone that comes near him.

Of these two, one might be labeled conservative,

the other progressive, but in actual fact there is not too much difference between them in so far as they are both operating under constraint. Now it would be disastrous if the liturgical renewal were to rely on the replacement of one kind of constraint by the other. Renewal means, on the contrary, the replacement of constraint by the openness of simple and joyous participation. Those who have emotional conflicts—and after all, who doesn't?—will do best if they can realize that this openness is practically the only thing that can ease their anxieties in this particular sphere. It will help them, by humility, grace, self-forgetfulness and trust to approach the Lord who will heal them in the relaxed and expanded atmosphere of love which is ideally that of Liturgical Worship.

I say "ideally" because the great problem we face in liturgy today is the temptation to discouragement and resentment which arises when the ideal is not only not promptly realized but not even approximated.

Those whom we may call progressives, whether in liturgy or in the whole field of Catholic renewal, may find themselves pushing forward blindly and recklessly, defying what seems to them an unfair spirit of resistance and inertia on the part of others. The "conservatives" meanwhile—and one regrets to say this—have at times been childishly rebellious to all change and have obstructed even the simplest and most obviously desirable adjustments. (Probably every town has an example of passive resistance and overt recrimination on the part of some Catholic prophet of doom who is now convinced that the

Church has become "Protestant" because people pray in English!)

Let us frankly realize that our task is precisely this: to demonstrate our elementary charity and un-selfishness—indeed our Christian maturity—by set-ting aside our own preferences (whether progressive or conservative) in order to arrive at some working formula by which we can all continue to worship as one in Christ. Let us also frankly admit that the tan-trums of extremists on both sides are, in most cases, simply childish.

Even well-balanced, sincere and naturally open people may find that the adaptation will not be en-tirely without struggle. In all social living there has to be a painful dialectic between programs and achieve-ments, ideals and realities, intention and execution. We may start out with a generous response to the program and its demands. We may really open up in all innocence and trust, forgetting that to be open is to be vulnerable. There is no choice, we cannot get into the real inner meaning of participation unless we let our guard down. But if we do, we may find ourselves face to face with someone who has only seemed to let his guard down, and who is still looking for a chance to reinforce his own self-esteem by cut-ting other people down to size.

In monasteries there is the perennial problem of the novice who comes to choir ready to give his all in the glorious praise of God, and who is quickly and repeatedly made to realize that his contribution is not appreciated. He is caught and ground between the upper millstone of liturgical exhortation from the cantors and the nether millstone of his own energetic incapacity. With his heart wide open, he plunges into cataclysm. After six months, he is reduced to frustrated silence, or sings in a miserable, self-pitying falsetto for the rest of his life, lost to renewal, to progress, to liturgy and to anything else but the well-tried spirituality of cloistered victimhood.

What is to be done about such problems? There is no magic answer. But one thing is certain. If all our ardor and attention are concentrated on a liturgical *ideal,* then we will inevitably end by hurting, punishing and unnecessarily constraining the poor well-meaning flesh and blood individual who takes our exhortation seriously, and generously tries to give us what we seem to be asking. Let us think of ideals, but also, above all, of people—not people in the abstract but the ones with whom we worship.

If we are going to ask limited human beings to participate in the liturgy, then we must be content for a while with the imperfect participation we are going to get. It is not always going to be wonderful. It is probably going to be in some ways much less tranquil and edifying than the comparative order and serenity of the "old mass." The new liturgy may be in many ways a relief—but it is not necessarily going to attain at once to perfect harmony, order and beauty. Let us not make things worse by insisting that everything we attempt is at once "perfect"!

One thing that will inevitably aggravate the sense of constraint is the fact that the liturgy continues to be our official public prayer, authoritative and precisely regulated. It makes severe demands, not only

on the feelings, the imagination and the understanding of the participant, not only on his heart and will,
but even on his conscience. One of the agonizing
things about the liturgy, for certain priests, is the
exaggerated fear of making mistakes and therefore of
being guilty. This "rubrical paralysis" is what accounts for the ugliness and impropriety of so many
Masses. Do not blame the poor priest! God alone
understands the depth of his unspoken tribulation.
The fault lies probably with the seminaries. The
mere changing of Laws does nothing to remedy this
situation. On the contrary, it creates new problems:
one finds himself trying to fulfil new obligations
which he does not yet properly understand . . .

By now, however, all of us have probably made
enough mistakes in the "new Mass" to realize first of
all that it is not just a matter of being rubrically correct. And also all of us have had to make special adjustments to meet a special situation so that, without
being "innovators" exactly, we have at least had to
interpret the new rubrics in a reasonable and constructive personal way. Hence the complaints of pa-
rishioners who deplore the fact that "every pastor
has a different way of doing things" are not really to
be taken seriously. If these people had lived in the
Middle Ages, to which they perhaps think they look
back with nostalgia, they would have found far
more regional differences and apparent inconsist-
encies than they will ever see in twentieth century
Catholicism. In fact one might say that medieval
Catholicism, as it *really* was, manifested in some areas
a spirit of freedom that we would do well to recap-

ture if we could. (I hasten to add that not *all* the clerical freedom of the Middle Ages was worthy of imitation.)

The liturgical renewal is going to demand a great deal of experimentation. But how can we experiment under juridical constraint? It would seem that much of the renewal will have to be carried on in a spirit of informality and freedom, to some extent outside the framework of formal liturgical worship. The dry mass, for instance, and the informal prayer vigil offer many possibilities of free experiment, one would almost say of improvisation, which would be out of the question in formal liturgical service or in the administration of the Sacraments.

One last thought: the open approach in liturgy is perhaps forever beyond the capacity of those of us who have grown old in "closed" and rigid forms. But there are children. They will be in any case the ones to benefit from the liturgical reform. Why not let them, in the simplicity and inspired spontaneity which are their special gift, and guided by sensitive and alert adults, begin to sketch out the creative and original forms of the future liturgy for which we are all waiting?

I make this suggestion seriously, and without a trace of sentiment. Naturally I have no clear idea how it might be done. But childhood *is* the age of openness, simplicity, spontaneity, and honesty. Of course, today's child has been influenced by TV, and his openness has been tampered with in many other subtle ways.

There is much hope for liturgical renewal if it can

somehow be carried out in a spirit of *play*. Play is not flippant or inconsequential. It is a very serious and very necessary activity. It is in play that the human heart is at once open, engaged, joyous, serious and self-forgetful. The open, thoughtless, hieratic self-forget-fulness of play is more likely than anything else to provide a substitute for the self-concerned engross-ment of subjective concentration that has so far pro-vided the worshipper with his chief ground for seri-ousness in worship.

If our own children cannot help us discover a new liturgy, perhaps the new nations, the more primitive societies which are the children in the family of nations, will be the ones to lead us into the world of renewal. The African monasteries of Cistercians and Benedictines have already petitioned the Holy See for permission to use native instruments (especially drums) in their worship.

One thing that is certain to come out of Africa is the revival of the ancient liturgical art of *the dance*, traditionally a problem to western Christianity. This of course opens up tempting avenues of speculation. But it must be said that the world today needs forms of worship that are dynamic, colorful, rhythmic and full of disciplined and expressive movement. Whatever may be the outcome, it is in that direction that the success of full liturgical participation really lies.

[1964]

2

TIME AND THE LITURGY

The Liturgy accepts our common, everyday experience of time: sunrise, noonday, sunset; spring, summer, autumn, winter. There is no reason for the Church in her prayer to do anything else "with time," for the obvious reason that the Church has no quarrel with time. The Church is not fighting against time. The Christian does not, or at any rate need not, consider time an enemy. Time is not doing him any harm, time is not standing between him and anything he desires. Time is not robbing him of anything he treasures.

To understand the attitude of the Christian and of the Liturgy towards time we must have a profound understanding of Christian hope and Christian trust. Fundamentally the Christian is at peace with time because he is at peace with God. He need no longer be fearful and distrustful of time, because now he understands that time is not being used by a hostile "fate" to determine his life in some sense which he himself can never know, and for which he cannot adequately be prepared. Time has now come to terms with man's freedom. When man is not free from sin,

25

then time is his enemy because every moment is a
threat of destruction: every moment may be the one
in which the unreality which man has chosen, by
sinning, is brought face to face with cataclysmic re-
proof and is shown to be the fruit of servility, the
abnegation of freedom, the surrender to determina-
tion by forces lower than man.

But when man recovers, in Christ, the freedom of
the Sons of God, he lives in time *without predeter-
mination,* because grace will always protect his freedom against the tyranny of evil. The Christian then
knows that time does not murmur an implicit threat
of enslavement and final destruction. Time on the
contrary gives scope for his freedom and his love.
Time gives free play to gratitude and to that sacrifice
of praise which is the full expression of the Christian's sonship in the Spirit. In other words time does
not *limit* freedom, but gives it scope for its exercise
and for choice. Time for the Christian is then the
sphere of his spontaneity, a sacramental gift in which
he can allow his freedom to deploy itself in joy, in the
creative virtuosity of choice that is always blessed
with the full consciousness that God wants His sons to
be free, that He is glorified by their freedom. For
God takes pleasure not in dictating predetermined
solutions to providential riddles, but in giving man
the opportunity to choose and create for himself
solutions that are glorious in their very contingency.

Does this mean that all temporal acts and decisions
are despised and abandoned to an inscrutable divine
will while the Christian disports himself in a realm of
disembodied, abstract and purely spiritual "free-

dom"? No, on the contrary, even the most humble
and contingent decisions of earthly and temporal life
come to participate in this Christian realm of praise.

Hence the Christian is not afraid of the clock, nor
is he in cunning complicity with it. The Christian life
is not really a "victory over time" because time is not
and cannot be a real antagonist. Of course, the Christian life is a victory over death: but it is a victory
which accepts death and accepts the lapse of time that
inevitably leads to death. But it does this in a full
consciousness that death is in no sense a "triumph of
time." For the Christian, time is no longer the de-
vourer of all things. Christian worship is at peace
with time because the *lapse* of time no longer con-
cerns the Christian whose life is "hidden with Christ
in God."

The Liturgy also accepts the archetypal, natural
image of a "sacred time," a primordial time which
mysteriously recurs and is present in the very heart of
secular time. Whenever the Gospel is sung in the
Liturgy it begins with the formula "at that time" (*in
illo tempore*) and the formula, in effect, destroys the
passage of time, annuls all the time that has passed
since "then," for in the Liturgy the "then" of the
salvific actions of Christ is "now" in the redemptive
mystery of the Church's prayer. Hence, though "at
that time" may perhaps suggest something of the
"once upon a time" of fairy tales, it is in reality a
quite different dimension. It is not *out of time,* not
an escape from the flux and fall of life, but an affirmation of the fulness of life, present "now" as it was
"then," neither in time nor out of it. Change and

duration are not set apart by the Church as absolutes in themselves. They are not the measure of realities with which she is concerned. Yet she uses our familiar experience of time as the "matter" so to speak of a sacramental and sanctifying action. Time is transformed by the Church's blessing and prayer.

History itself acquired a new meaning, or rather its hidden meaning was revealed, when the Word of God became incarnate and entered into history. Time itself was now an Epiphany of the Creator and of the Redeemer, the "Lord of Ages." And yet time also acquired a new solemnity, a new urgency, since the Lord Himself now declared that time would have an end.

We live in the kingdom of Christ, the new world, consecrated to God, the messianic kingdom, the new Jerusalem. The history of the kingdom is working itself out, but in the mystery of faith, hidden from the wise of this world (I Cor. 1:19–21) and the final day of its manifestation is reserved for the future—the end of time.

Time, which is now enclosed between the two advents of Christ—His first coming in humility and obscurity, and His second coming in majesty and power—has been claimed by God for His own. Time is to be sanctified like everything else, by the presence and the action of Christ.

The redemption is not simply a past historical fact with a juridical effect on individual souls. It is an ever present reality, living and efficacious, penetrating the inmost depths of our being by the word of salvation and the mystery of faith. The redemption is

Christ Himself, "who of God is made to us wisdom and justice and sanctification and redemption" (I Cor. 1:30) living and sharing His divine life with His elect. To be redeemed is not merely to be absolved of guilt before God, it is also to live in Christ, to be born again of water and the Holy Spirit, to be in Him a new creature, to live in the Spirit.

To say that the redemption is an ever present spiritual reality is to say that Christ has laid hold upon time and sanctified it, giving it a sacramental character, making it an efficacious sign of our union with God in Him. So "time" is a medium which makes the fact of redemption present to all men.

Christ has given a special meaning and power to the cycle of the seasons, which of themselves are "good" and by their very nature have a capacity to signify our life in God: for the seasons express the rhythm of natural life. They are the systole and diastole of the natural life of our globe. Jesus has made this ebb and flow of light and darkness, activity and rest, birth and death, the sign of a higher life, a life which we live in Him, a life which knows no decline, and a day which does not fall into darkness. It is the "day of the Lord" which dawns for us anew each morning, the day of Easter, the "eighth day," the *Pascha Domini,* the day of eternity, shining upon us in time.

For fallen and unredeemed man, the cycle of seasons, the wheel of time itself, is only a spiritual prison. Each new spring brings a temporary hope. Autumn and winter destroy that hope with their ever returning reminder of death. For man living only in the flesh, only on the level of his nature, for man living without God, the great realities of human love and fertility are without issue. We are begotten by parents who disappear from the face of the earth and are forgotten. In our own turn, we grow, become strong, bring forth sons, and then we too fail, and die and are forgotten. Our sons in their turn will pass through the same cycle which ends inexorably in death, and in oblivion.

It is as if the whole of nature were striving upwards, but striving in vain. Generation after generation she kindles the flames of countless human spirits, capable of an eternal destiny, lives that have insatiable aspirations for love, for wisdom, for joy in God. The flames leap up for a brief moment, then die down and are extinguished. They are followed by others. None of them can reach up into eternity. The cycle of the seasons reminds us, by this perpetual renewal and perpetual death, that death is the end of all. The universe which came into being will some day grow cold, perhaps, and die. What will remain? Such is the view of life and time implied by the Hellenistic mystery religions, with their ontological foundations in Platonism. Time, the realm of matter and of "becoming" is the prison of eternal and divine spirits who have been punished by their descent into bodies, and seek desperately some way to return to the pure spiritual realm which is their "home." This climate of dualism and myth has, in effect, influenced much Christian thought, though it is not found in the Bible.

The modern pagan, the child of technology or the

"mass man," does not even enjoy the anguish of dualism or the comfort of myth. His anxieties are no longer born of eternal aspiration, though they are certainly rooted in a consciousness of death. "Mass man" is something more than fallen. He lives not only below the level of grace, but below the level of nature—below his own humanity. No longer in contact with the created world or with himself, out of touch with the reality of nature, he lives in the world of collective obsessions, the world of systems and fictions with which modern man has surrounded himself. In such a world, man's life is no longer even a seasonal cycle. It's a linear flight into nothingness, a flight from reality and from God, without purpose and without objective, except to keep moving, to keep from having to face reality. (See Max Picard: *The Flight from God.*)

To live in Christ we must first break away from this linear flight into nothingness and recover the rhythm and order of man's real nature. Before we can become gods we must first be men.

For man in Christ, the cycle of the seasons is something entirely new. It has become a *cycle of salvation.* The year is not just another year, it is the *year of the Lord*—a year in which the passage of time itself brings us not only the natural renewal of spring and the fruitfulness of an earthly summer, but also the spiritual and interior fruitfulness of grace. The life of the flesh which ebbs and flows like the seasons and tends always to its last decline is elevated and supplanted by a life of the spirit which knows no decrease, which always grows in those who live with

Christ in the liturgical year. "For though the outward man is corrupted, yet the inward man is renewed day by day. . . . For we know if our earthly house of this habitation be dissolved that we have a building of God, a house not made with hands, eternal in heaven." (II Cor. 4:16; 5:1)

The Word of God having entered into time by His birth of a Virgin Mother, has changed the cycle of the seasons from an imprisonment to a liberation. The Church prays God, at Christmas, that "the new birth of Thy only begotten Son may set us free, whom the old bondage detains under the yoke of sin."

The liturgy makes the very passage of time sanctify our lives, for each new season renews an aspect of the great Mystery of Christ living and present in His Church. Each recurring season shows us some new way in which we live in Him, in which He acts in the world. Each new feast draws our attention to the great truth of His presence in the midst of us, and shows us a different aspect of the Paschal Mystery in our world, now in the temporal cycle, and again in His saints, now in His sacraments, and again in the hallowed building of His churches, in His altars, and in the relics of His saints.

The liturgical cycle renews our redemption in Christ, delivers us from the servitude of sin and from the corruption of a "fleshly" mode of being. The liturgical cycle shows us that though we are caught in a struggle between flesh and spirit, though we are indeed the "fighting Church"—the Church militant—yet the victory is already ours. We possess the grace of Christ, who alone can deliver us from the "body of this death." He who is in us is stronger than the world. He has "overcome the world." In the cycle of the holy year, the Church rhythmically breathes the life-giving atmosphere of the Spirit, and her bloodstream is cleansed of the elements of death. She lives in Christ, and with Him praises the Father.

And so, while the cycle of time is a prison without escape for the natural man, living "in the flesh," and doomed to disappear with all the rest of his world that passes away, and while time is for the man of our cities only a linear flight from God, for the believer who lives in Christ each new day renews his participation in the mystery of Christ. Each day is a new dawn of that *lumen Christi,* the light of Christ which knows no setting.

The liturgical year renews the mysteries of our redemption each day in the Mass and Divine Office. It renews our participation in particular mysteries of the life of Christ. It teaches us the ways of the saints and renews our union with them in the charity of the Spirit. It is a year of *salvation,* but also a year of *enlightenment* and of *transformation.*

The mysteries of the liturgical cycle not only bring new outpourings of the salvific waters of grace: they also enlighten our minds with insights into the ways of God, ever ancient and ever new. They teach us more of Christ, they show us more of the meaning of our life in Him, they make us grow in Him, they transform us in Him. Indeed, the liturgy is the great school of Christian living and the transforming force which reshapes our souls and our characters in the likeness of Christ.

Dom Odo Casel compared the liturgical year to a ring which the Church, the virgin bride of Christ, triumphantly displays as the sign of her union with the incarnate Word. This holy ring is the gift of Christ to His Church as a pledge of His love and of His fidelity to His promises. The "cycle" or "circle" of the liturgy, which eternally returns to its beginning, is a symbol of the unity of God who is eternally the same yet ever new.

More than that, however, the liturgical "ring" of feasts is a symbol of that first "cycle" of actions by which Christ redeemed the world—the "ring" created by His descent into time, His life, death, resurrection and ascension into heaven restoring all things, in Himself, to the Father.

"The Father Himself loveth you because you have loved Me and have believed that I came forth from the Father. I came forth from the Father and am come into the world: again, I leave the world and I go to the Father." (John 16:28)

These words of St John show us that the Church's belief in Christ is not a mere static assent to His historical existence, but a dynamic participation in the great cycle of actions which manifest in the world the love of the Father for the ones He has called to union with Himself, in His beloved Son. It is not simply that we are "saved," and that the Father remits the debt contracted by our sins, but that we are *loved* by the Father, and loved by Him in so far as we believe that He has sent His Son, and has called Him back into heaven after having given all power into His hands.

In the liturgical year, the Church sees and acclaims

this action of the Father who so loved the world that He gave His only begotten Son for the salvation of men. It is a dialogue between mankind and the Father, in which the Father manifests Himself in His Word, and in which the Church, filled with the Spirit of the Father and the Son, praises and magnifies the glory of the Father, together with the Son.

To enter into the liturgical cycle is to participate in the great work of redemption effected by the Son. "Liturgy" is "common work"—a sacred work in which the Church cooperates with the divine Redeemer in re-living His mysteries and applying their fruits to all mankind.

It is quite clear that the Church does not regard the liturgy as a mere source of aesthetic satisfaction, or as an expression of Christian culture which stimulates devotion and piety. Nor is it merely a way in which the Christian society becomes formally aware of its existence and its relationship to God, in order to praise Him. It is a *work* in which the Church collaborates with the divine Redeemer, renewing on her altars the sacred mysteries which are the life and salvation of man, uttering again the life-giving words that are capable of saving and transforming our souls, blessing again the sick and the possessed, and preaching His Gospel to the poor.

In the liturgy, then, the Church would have us realize that we meet the same Christ who went about everywhere doing good, and who is still present in the midst of us wherever two or three are gathered together in His name. And we meet Him by sharing in His life and His redemption. We meet Christ in order to *be* Christ and, with Him, save the world.

In order to understand the full meaning of the liturgy we have to grasp the liturgical conception of time.

The Christian "present" of the liturgy has something of the character of eternity, in which all reality is present at once. The past and the future are therefore made present in the mysteries of the liturgy. In the Advent mystery, the Church not only re-lives the longing of the prophets and the patriarchs for the Redeemer, not only prays to God for the grace of a "new nativity" at Christmas, but also anticipates the coming of Christ at the Last Day. In every liturgical mystery the Church embraces the whole history of man's salvation, while concentrating her attention, for the time being, on one particular moment of that history.

At Christmas, we celebrate the coming of God into the world. We look especially at His birth at Bethlehem and see how that birth reveals to us the infinite mercy of God. But at the same moment we return to the very beginning of all. The generation of the Word in the bosom of the Father is also present to us, and we go forward to the end of all when, having come again into the world at the Last Judgment, and taken all things to Himself, and made all things new, we ourselves will share, by glory, in His divine and eternal sonship and hear the voice of the Father saying to us, in Him: "This day have I begotten thee!"

In every liturgical mystery we have this telescoping of time and eternity, of the universal and the personal, what is common to all ages, what is above and beyond all time and place, and what is most particular and most immediate to our own time and place. Christ in His infinite greatness embraces all things, the divine and the human, the spiritual and the material, the old and the new, the great and the small, and in the liturgy He makes Himself all things to all men and becomes all in all.

The works which Christ accomplished in time remain in eternity, treasured in the Sacred Heart from which they came forth, and the liturgical mysteries make these works present to us each time they are celebrated. Not only that, the liturgy incorporates us in His mysteries and renews their effect in time and in space. By the liturgy, while remaining in time, we enter into the great celebration that takes place before the throne of the Lamb in heaven, in eternity. As the Church prays, "as often as this saving Victim is offered up, so often the work of our redemption is carried out." (Secret, ninth Sunday after Pentecost)

Liturgy respects the flow of time and of history and yet, because it is in the "fulness of time," it anticipates the final accomplishment of all that time means to the Church. Time is "baptized" and sanctified by the infusion of the divine light hidden in the liturgical mysteries, a light which flows forth to penetrate our living and our actions and to fill them with the presence of the Lord Christ, the *Kyrios Christos.*

In each new liturgical feast we celebrate Christ Himself, not just the various things which He did, or the exploits of His saints. At Christmas, we celebrate Christ, living and present to us in Mystery, and commune with the divine mercy that He manifests by His birth. At the Epiphany we celebrate Christ as

present among us, diffusing upon the world the light
and glory of the Father and making known the
Father's plan for the salvation of the gentiles. At
Septuagesima we return to the creation of the world,
in the Word, who is present with us: we consider
flight from God into the darkness of sin. We share
with Christ the labors and sufferings of His public
life in Lent; then we enter into His passion. In Holy
Week, Christ is present in the midst of His Church as
the Lamb slain before the beginning of the world, as
the Servant of Yahweh whose sufferings were foretold
by Isaias and Jeremias, as the Christ who is crucified
even today in His holy Church. At Easter, He is
present among us as risen and triumphant, and shed-
ding upon us the light of eternal peace. At Pentecost
He is present among us as the founder of His Church
and the giver of the Paraclete Who manifests Him in
His Church.

In all these liturgical seasons, as Dom Gueranger
says, "Christ Himself is the source as well as the
object of the liturgy. Hence the ecclesiastical year is
neither more nor less than the manifestation of Jesus
Christ in His mysteries, in the Church, and in the
faithful soul. It is the divine cycle in which appear all
the works of God, each in its turn . . . If every year
the Church renews her youth as that of the eagle, she
does so by means of the cycle of the liturgy; she is
visited by her divine Spouse who supplies all her
wants." (*Liturgical Year,* Vol. 1, 9–10)

Pope Pius XII canonized these teachings in the
succinct formulas of *Mediator Dei:*

Throughout the entire year, the Mass and the divine office center especially around the Person of Jesus Christ . . . When the sacred liturgy calls to mind the mysteries of Jesus Christ, it strives to make all believers take their part in them so that the divine Head of the Mystical Body may live in all the members with the fulness of His holiness. Let the souls of Christians be like altars on each of which a different phase of the Sacrifice of the High Priest comes to life again . . . Hence the liturgical year . . . is not a cold and lifeless representation of the events of the past, or a bare and simple record of a former age; it is rather *Christ Himself who is ever living in His Church.* (151, 152, 165)

But if Christ is "ever present" in the Liturgy of the Church, and if the Liturgical cycle is an "ever recurring" cycle of feasts, does this not imply a return to the old concept of cyclical time, the "myth of the eternal return?" Does this not re-establish us firmly in the ancient cycle of seasons, and does it not finally reduce the Christian liturgy to a glorified and spiritualized cult of natural fecundity and rebirth?

It is true that the myths and symbols of archaic worship have to some extent left their mark on Christian symbolism since the days when the Gospel was preached in the world of Greece and Rome. Nevertheless, all Christianity that is true to its origins preserves the purity and simplicity of that eschatological vision which makes time utterly transparent, for all time has now become "the time of the end."*

---

* Gunther Anders has coined this striking expression to describe the change of perspective that followed the dropping of the first Atomic Bomb on Hiroshima. We are now living in an age in

But in proportion as we regard our Christian life as the canonization of merely temporal and social patterns, and as we place our hopes in a Christianity fully rooted and established not in Christ Himself, regardless of time, but in time "with the approval of Christ," we will have an entirely different concept of Liturgy and of Christianity, we will make our worship the reflection and glorification of the institutional structures in which we imagine our temporal hope to be made secure.

Liturgical time loses its meaning when it becomes simply the complacent celebration of the *status quo,* and if the "present" of liturgy is merely the "given" situation in which we find our human security. The paradox of liturgical time is that it is humanly insecure, seeking its peace altogether outside the structures of all that is established, visible and familiar, in the hope of a Kingdom which is not seen. It is that hope and that alone that makes Christ present among us. Outside that eschatological hope there is no meaning and no dynamism in liturgical worship.

[1955]

---

which we *know* that the world can at any moment be rendered practically uninhabitable, and mankind obliterated. Yet in a very real sense this consciousness was already that of the first Christians. One is tempted to speculate on the profound effect the Christian eschatological concept of time has had on all subsequent developments in thought and science.

3

ADVENT: HOPE
OR DELUSION?

The certainty of Christian hope lies beyond passion and beyond knowledge. Therefore we must sometimes expect our hope to come in conflict with darkness, desperation and ignorance. Therefore, too, we must remember that Christian optimism is not a perpetual sense of euphoria, an indefectible comfort in whose presence neither anguish nor tragedy can possibly exist. We must not strive to maintain a climate of optimism by the mere *suppression* of tragic realities. Christian optimism lies in a hope of victory that transcends all tragedy: a victory in which we *pass beyond* tragedy to glory with Christ crucified and risen.

It is important to remember the deep, in some ways anguished seriousness of Advent, when the mendacious celebrations of our marketing culture so easily harmonize with our tendency to regard Christmas, consciously or otherwise, as a return to our own innocence and our own infancy. Advent should remind us that the "King Who is to Come" is more than a charming infant smiling (or if you prefer a dolorous spirituality, weeping) in the straw. There is certainly nothing wrong with the traditional family joys of Christmas, nor need we be ashamed to find ourselves still able to anticipate them without too much ambivalence. After all, that in itself is no mean feat.

But the Church in preparing us for the birth of a "great prophet," a Savior and a King of Peace, has more in mind than seasonal cheer. The Advent mystery focuses the light of faith upon the very meaning of life, of history, of man, of the world and of our own being. In Advent we celebrate the coming and indeed the *presence* of Christ in our world. We witness to His presence even in the midst of all its inscrutable problems and tragedies. Our Advent faith is not an escape from the world to a misty realm of slogans and comforts which declare our problems to be unreal, our tragedies inexistent.

The Advent Gospels, like most of the other liturgical texts of the season, are sober to the point of austerity. Take for example the question of St John the Baptist in Herod's prison, where he was about to undergo a tragic death that was at once cruel and senseless: "Are you He who is to come, or look we for another?" Strange and even scandalous words, which some have never been able to accept at their face value! How can John have meant such a question, when he had seen the Holy Spirit descending upon Jesus in the Jordan? Yet the directness with which the question was asked was the guarantee of its desperate seriousness: for at the close of his life, John was concerned not only, as we might say, for the "success of his mission" but more profoundly still, for the *truth of his own life, the truth of Israel,* indeed the *truth of Yahweh Himself.*

In our time, what is lacking is not so much the courage to ask this question as the courage to expect an answer. There are enough men, some of them great men, who think that the only authentic posture is the frank acceptance of hopelessness in the face of life. Perhaps one reason why Sartre takes this position is that he feels Christians are always giving themselves a cozy answer to a desperate question they do not have the courage to ask. In which case our glad acceptance of the answer may be something less than edifying.

St Gregory the Great said that all Christians should continue the prophetic mission of John and point out the presence of Christ in the world. This may mean many different things. John was able to point out Christ at the Jordan, in a moment of fulfillment, which gave meaning to his whole life. But John also had to witness to Christ in prison, in face of death, in failure, when even the meaning of his other glorious moment seemed to have been cancelled out.

So too, we may at times be able to show the world Christ in moments when all can clearly discern in history, some confirmation of the Christian message. But the fact remains that our task is to seek and find Christ in our world as it is, and not as it *might be.* The fact that the world is other than it might be does not alter the truth that Christ is present in it and that His plan has been neither frustrated nor changed: indeed, all will be done according to His will. Our Advent is the celebration of this hope. What is uncertain is not the "coming" of Christ but our own reception of Him, our own response to Him, our own readiness and capacity to "go forth to meet Him." We must be willing to see Him and acclaim Him, as John did, even at the very moment when our whole life's work and all its meaning seem to collapse. Indeed, more formidable still, the Church herself may perhaps be called upon some day to point out the Victorious Redeemer and King of Ages amid the collapse of all that has been laboriously built up by the devotion of centuries and cultures that sincerely intended to be Christian.

The Advent of Christ in history is not essentially bound up with the development and progress of a Christian *civilization*. "Christendom" is, and has been a great thing, but it has never been an absolute and unqualified good or an end in itself. *Christendom* is not *Christianity*. It is not "the Kingdom" and it is not the Mystical Christ.

The reality of Christian culture certainly flows from the presence of Christ in the world, but it is not identical with that presence. Our Advent is, then, not a celebration of mere traditional cultural values, however great, however worthy of perpetuation. Advent is not a mere return, a recurrence, and a renewal of the old. It cannot be a return to childhood, whether personal or social. The coming of the Lord, which is the same as His "presence" is the coming of the new, not the renewal of the old, and Sacred History is like the Heraklitean river in which no man steps twice.

Yet, since the Kingdom is the "fullness of time" it

does in some sense make the past present in its fulfillment. But the past fulfilled is not the past, it is not
merely renewed, it is completely transformed into the
present. Baptism is the fulfillment of the Exodus, not
its commemoration. The Eucharist is the Sacrifice of
the Lord made present in its eternal reality, not re-
enacted in a ritual drama which revives the past.
These sacred realities have a kind of timelessness: not
that they are static and eternal ideas, Platonic ab-
stractions, but dynamic fulfillment of all that is temporal and incomplete. Thus they can at the same
instant enter time and transcend it.

John's question: "Are you He who is to come?"
contains a curious telescoping of time. The present
merges with the future, and there is also a suggestion
of the past, since it refers back to John's previous
testimony that in Christ the Savior of the world had
already come. Our own celebration of Advent contains this same curious telescoping of past, present
and future. We not only believe that Christ "will
come" but also that He "has come." And this focuses
our attention upon the present in which, as far as
human evidence is concerned, there may or may not
be some visible sign of either.

Yet we believe that He who has come and will
come is present here and now: that we are in His
Kingdom. Not only that, but we *are* His Kingdom.
And I think that explains why we are not always too
happy about asking John's question, since it implies a
questioning of ourselves, of our life, of our part in
history, of the very meaning of the mystery of Christ
in His Church. Surely, we believe that Christ is in us,

that He lives and acts in the world because He is present in the Church. And we are His Church. But what does this mean? Is this presence something "purely spiritual"? If it is so "spiritual" that it has absolutely no visible or meaningful effect in contemporary society, we might as well admit it has no meaning that our contemporaries are likely to be interested in. Shall we adopt this position, and write our contemporaries off as contumacious heathen ready for the flames of Gehenna? Or do they have a right to ask *of us* this perilous question: "Are *you* the Kingdom of Christ Who is come, the Prince of Peace, the Just One, the Messiah who comes to bring unity and peace to the divided world of man?"

Do they have a right to *see* in us some evidence of the presence and action of Christ, some visible manifestation of the *Pneuma?* Surely it is not impertinent of them to ask to be shown what we claim is present in us. And this claim is not a matter of esoteric and perilous theologies. Our favorite apologetic argument for the divine mission of Christ is the holiness of the Church. But how evident does holiness have to be? Where, with what frequency, and how incontestably does it have to be manifest? Is it sufficient that we should be the only ones to be aware that we are holy?

How shall we answer such questions or even dare to ask them, unless we understand the kenotic quality of the Advent mystery? The Christ who emptied Himself taking the form of a servant, dying on the Cross for us, brought us the plenitude of His gifts and of His salvation. But He continues in us a kenotic and hidden existence. The fullness of time is the time of His emptiness in us. The fullness of time is the time of our emptiness, which draws Christ down into our lives so that in us and through us He may bring the fullness of His truth to the world.

Here is where we must beware of our own biased concepts of "fullness" and of "fulfillment." It is true that the glory and the presence of Christ have sometimes visibly overflowed not only in spiritual charismata, but also in what one might call the charism of culture and the spiritual forms of *civiltà*. But obviously this "charism" is at best metaphorical or analogous, since it involves the "baptising" of forms that are very limited both in time and in geography. The more we are "full" with these fulfillments, and the more we identify the countenance of a prosperous culture with the face of the glorified *Kyrios,* the more we tend to be deceived by projection and wish-fulfillment, the greater the danger that our Christianity will become a vain "boast" in the sight of God. In such a case, the Advent of the Lord demands nothing more or less than a return to the "emptiness" of faith. It may even mean the destruction of the false image which we had set up in honor of our own achievement or which, set up in honor of the Lord, was yet not worthy of Him.

If the Lord wishes to live in us His self-emptying, His kenosis, it is not likely that He will tolerate in us the fullness and self-congratulation of collective arrogance. Upon whom will His Spirit rest but upon the humble and the poor? This does not mean that occasional or even widespread pride may validly cast doubts upon the truth of the Church: but it does mean that the strength and holiness of the Church are not, at that moment, where they are supposed and claimed to be. Indeed, it may happen that the best Christians are among those who think themselves for some reason or other bad Christians. This, too, may be part of the mystery of Advent, and it can remind us of Christ's way, as recorded in the Gospels: He came most readily and most willingly to those who had most need of Him, that is to the unfortunate, the sinful, the destitute—those who were "empty."

The Advent mystery is then a mystery of emptiness, of poverty, of limitation. It must be so. Otherwise it could not be a mystery of hope. The Advent mystery is a mystery of beginning: but it is also the mystery of an end. The fullness of time is the end of all that was not yet fullness. It is the completion of all that was still incomplete, all that was still partial. It is the fulfillment in oneness of all that was fragmentary.

The Advent mystery in our own lives is the beginning of the end of all, in us, that is not yet Christ. It is the beginning of the end of unreality. And that is surely a cause of joy! But unfortunately we cling to our unreality, we prefer the part to the whole, we continue to be fragments, we do not want to be "one man in Christ."

Theologically, since human nature was assumed by the Word of God in Christ, all humanity is at least potentially "the humanity of Christ" in the sense that every existing human nature belongs by right, and indeed in fact, to Christ. Hence the terrible truth that a mankind which belongs to Christ without perhaps knowing it, or without being able to really evaluate the meaning of so astonishing a mystery, is spiritually alienated from Him and is tearing itself to pieces.

The Body of Adam ("Man"), which should be the Body of God's Love, is torn with hate. The Body of Adam which should be transfigured with light, is a Body of obscurity and untruth. That which should be One in love is divided into millions of frenzied and murderous hostilities. Yet the fact remains: Christ the King of Peace has come into the world and saved it. He has saved Man, He has established His Kingdom, and His Kingdom is the Kingdom of Peace. Furthermore, *we* are His Kingdom. Yet we have devised a power capable of destroying not cities, not nations, but *Man*. "Are you He Who is to come, or look we for another?"

Christ, in answering John's disciples, gave them signs which, according to the preaching of the Old Testament prophets, were clear indication that the Messianic Kingdom had come. They were also indications that the "fullness of time" had come and that the old world had ended. These were the "last days," the days of fulfillment, the days of "the end" because they were days of the "beginning."

Advent for us means acceptance of this totally new beginning. It means a readiness to have eternity and time meet not only in Christ but *in us,* in Man, in our life, in our world, in our time. If we are to enter into the beginning of the new, we must accept the death of the old. The beginning, therefore, is the end. We must accept the end, before we can begin. Or rather, to be more faithful to the complexity of life, we must accept the end in the beginning, both together.

The secret of the Advent mystery is then the awareness that I begin where I end because Christ begins where I end. In more familiar terms: I live to Christ when I die to myself. I begin to live to Christ when I come to the "end" or to the "limit" of what divides me from my fellow man: when I am willing to step beyond this end, cross the frontier, become a stranger, enter into the wilderness which is not "myself," where I do not breathe the air or hear the familiar, comforting racket of my own city, where I am alone and defenseless in the desert of God.

The victory of Christ is by no means the victory of my city over "their" city. The exaltation of Christ is not the defeat and death of others in order that "my side" may be vindicated, that I may be proved "right." I must pass over, make the transition (*pascha*) from my end to my beginning, from my old life which has ended and which is now death to my new life which never was before and which now exists in Christ.

Christ's answer to the disciples of John was the answer of newness and of life: "Go and tell John what you have seen: the blind see, the lame walk, and the poor have the Gospel preached to them." Here are two kinds of eschatological signs, and they compenetrate one another, for they are all signs of life, proceeding from love. Evil ends, and gives place to good in a physical and visible way: blindness ends, sight begins. Sickness ends, health begins. Death ends, life begins. But all these signs are evidence of an inexhaustible living power, the action of Life Itself, bursting into time, defeating and reversing the work of time. Hence this power manifests the "fullness of time," in which time is no longer mere irreversible succession, mere passage from insufficiency to insufficiency. Above all, the raising of the dead is a reversal and a conquest of time: for normally when the "hour of death" has struck, there can never again be an "hour of life." Yet the "hour" of Christ, when it struck, was at once the hour of death, of victory, of life and of glory. "Father the hour has come, glorify your Son that your Son may glorify You."

More important than the eschatological sign of renewed physical life is the sign *par excellence:* "The Gospel is preached to the poor." This means that the prophetic message of salvation, the fulfillment of the divine promises is now formally announced to the *anawim,* to those who hungered and thirsted for the Kingdom because they had no hope but the Lord. And therefore the last days have come. It is the end, because the fulfillment which earth and time could not give, is now at hand. This fulfillment has begun because now Christ has appeared in the midst of the poor as one of them, and has taken them to Himself so that they are, in a most special way, Himself. What happens to them happens, in a very particular way, to Him. (Matt. 25:37-45. Cf. Matt. 5:3-6, 10, 11) The Last Days have come not merely because the poor have *heard about* Christ but because they "are" Christ. The poor themselves now become an eschatalogical sign of Christ, a sign by which other men are judged, for *"if the wicked servant says in his heart:*

*'My Lord delays in coming' and begins to strike his
fellow servants,* and eats and drinks with drunkards,
the Lord of that servant will come on the day he does
not expect and in the hour which he does not know,
and will cut him off (from Man in Christ) and give
him his portion with the hypocrites." (Matthew
24:48–50)

The mystery of Advent, therefore, centers in the
fact that *God is now present in Man, and men will be
judged according to their acceptance of this crucial
truth,* in all its consequences. What we do to man, we
do to Christ, the God-man. Hence the tragedy of
contemporary disorders and injustice. It is not only
that they prevent men from becoming one in Christ,
but rather that they rend mankind in pieces when, in
the Advent Mystery, Man already *is* at least inchoa-
tively, one in Christ!

In the light of current events, this is a sobering if
not a frightening doctrine. Who of us does not fail in
this faith? But there is hope in St Paul's famous text:
Whether well or badly, we all build on one foundation, Christ Jesus. No other foundation stone can be
laid down. We can build on this foundation with
gold, or stone, or wood, or straw. In the Day of the
Lord (the day, that is, of His "Advent"), each one's
work will be tried by fire. "If any man's work remain,
which he has built on the foundation, he will receive
a reward. If a man's work burns, he suffers loss, He
himself shall be saved: saved, however, as though by
fire." I Cor. 3:14–15.)

This is the "tragic" aspect of the Advent mystery
for sincere and faithful Christians. We do, indeed,

love Christ. We are among those who, in St Paul's
phrase, "love His coming (Advent)" (2 Tim. 4:8).
We work for Him, and for His Kingdom. But we are
also blind, confused, weak, fallible. We have resisted,
perhaps sometimes even extinguished His Spirit, and
done so perhaps when we thought we were most
zealous for His truth. There have been great mistakes. Heroic efforts have been sometimes made and
wasted. When times of crisis come to shake us out of
our complacency, this all becomes sadly evident.
What then shall we say? Advent, in these sombre
years of "wars and rumors of wars" reminds us that
though our work may be judged, and found wanting,
even totally consumed by fire, it is in the very fire
that destroys our imperfect works that we ourselves
can be saved.

[1963]

4

THE NATIVITY KERYGMA

NOTE: Christianity is not so much a body of doctrine as the revelation of a mystery. A mystery is a divine action, something which God does in time in order to introduce men into the sanctuary of eternity. Being a religion of mysteries, Christianity is a religion of facts—divine facts, divine actions.

In celebrating the mysteries of Christ as they recur in time, the Church first of all announces these events: "Christ is born!" "Christ is risen!" She proclaims them, as a herald proclaims the triumphal entrance of a victorious King into a city. Her announcement, her proclamation of the divine event, is a work which she entrusts to her "heralds," her apostles, her preachers. Christianity is thus essentially kerygmatic: the priest is a herald, *kerux*, an angel of the Lord of Hosts, a voice crying out in the desert: "Make straight the ways of the Lord."

These pages are a proclamation, a *kerygma*, of the nativity of the Son of God, Our Lord and Savior Jesus Christ. They announce the fact of His birth. They proclaim the presence of His mystery among us *now*, this year. They say, as the Church also says in her liturgy, "This day, Christ is born, this day the Savior has ap-

peared: this day the angels sing on earth and the arch-
angels rejoice: this day the just exult, saying: Glory to
God in the highest, alleluia."

Christ is born. He is born *to us*. And, He is born
today. For Christmas is not merely a day like every
other day. It is a day made holy and special by a
sacred mystery. It is not merely another day in the
weary round of time. Today, eternity enters into
time, and time, sanctified, is caught up into eternity.
Today, Christ, the Eternal Word of the Father, Who
was in the beginning with the Father, in whom all
things were made, by whom all things consist, enters
into the world which He created in order to reclaim
souls who had forgotten their identity. Therefore, the
Church exults, as the angels come down to announce
not merely an old thing which happened long ago,
but a new thing which happens today. For, today,
God the Father makes all things new, in His Divine
Son, our Redeemer, according to His words: *ecce
nova facio omnia*.

Therefore, the Church on earth joins with the
Church in heaven to sing one same song, the new
song, the *canticum novum* which the Prophet commanded all to sing after the world should have been
redeemed by the Christ, Whose ancestor he knew, by
revelation, that he should be. When David cried out:
"Sing to the Lord a new song," he was the first pre-
centor to intone the songs the Church would sing on
this day in her liturgy, as she announces to the whole
world salvation and joy. For, as Saint Leo says: "Today there has shone upon us a day of new redemp-

tion, a day restoring that which was long lost, a day of bliss unending."

So, with the *Alleluia* of victory, the triumphant cry of Easter on her lips, the Church renews the Paschal mystery in which death is conquered, the power of the devil is broken forever, and sins are forgiven: the mystery of the death and resurrection of the Savior who is born to us on this day. Today, the Church sings: *Dies sanctificatus illuxit nobis,* which means: A day of salvation, a day sanctified by mystery, a day full of divine and sanctifying power, has shone upon us. And she continues: *"Alleluia, Alleluia:* A sanctified day has shone upon us: come you gentiles and adore the Lord: for this day a great light has descended upon the earth." The Church summons all the world to adoration as she prepares with great solemnity to announce the words of the Gospel in her third Mass. This is the Prologue of John, in which with mighty power given him from God the greatest Evangelist proclaims that the Word, Who was in the beginning with God, is made flesh, and dwells among us full of grace and truth.

At Christmas, more than ever, it is fitting to remember that we have no other light but Christ, Who is born to us today. Let us reflect that He came down from heaven to be our light, and our life. He came, as He Himself assures us, to be our way, by which we may return to the Father. Christ gives us light today to know Him, in the Father and ourselves in Him, that, thus, knowing and possessing Christ, we may have life everlasting with Him in the Father. "For this is eternal life, that they may know Thee, Father,

the one True God, and Jesus Christ, whom Thou
has sent" and again, "As many as received Him He
gave them the power to be made the sons of God."

Having realized, once again, Who it is that comes
to us, and having remembered that He alone is our
light let us open our eyes to the rising Sun, let us
hasten to receive Him and let us come together to
celebrate the great mystery of charity which is the
sacrament of our salvation and of our union in
Christ. Let us receive Christ that we may in all truth
be "light in the Lord" and that Christ may shine not
only *to* us, but *through* us, and that we may all burn
together in the sweet light of His presence in the
world: I mean His presence in us, for we are His
Body and His Holy Church.

As Saint Paul says (and we sing this in one of
the Epistles today): "In these days, God has spoken
to us in His Son, Whom He has appointed heir of all
things, by Whom also He made the world: Who
being the brightness of His glory and the figure of
His substance, and upholding all things by the word
of His power, making purgation of sins, sits on the
right hand of the majesty." And in another place the
same Apostle says: "God who commanded the light to
shine out of darkness has shined in our hearts, to give
the light of the glory of God in the face of Christ
Jesus."

Christ, light of light, is born today, and since He is
born to us, He is born in us as light and therefore, we
who believe are born today to new light. That is to
say, our souls are born to new life and new grace by
receiving Him who is the Truth. For Christ, invisible

in His own nature, has become visible in our nature. What else can this mean, except that first He has become visible as man and second He has become visible in His Church? He wills to be visible in us, to live in us, work in us, and save us through His secret action in our own hearts and the hearts of our brothers. So, we must receive the light of the newborn Savior by faith, in order to manifest it by our witness in common praise and by the works of our charity towards one another.

These two things, this witness and this charity, are united together in the greatest of all our acts of worship in which we celebrate together the divine mysteries, thus proclaiming our faith, renewing our eternal covenant with God our Father, and receiving into our midst Him Who is the fountainhead of our faith as well as its object. We give Him, as it were, to one another, in the fraternal charity which unites us in the bonds of peace. For after Christ has been born in our hearts, He reaches out to Himself in the heart of our brother by the love of His own Spirit. Binding Himself, as He is in us, with Himself, as He is in our brother, He restores us, in that same Holy Spirit, to the embrace of the heavenly Father.

We are born today in Christ, to this embrace and to this peace. Can it be surprising that we feel in our hearts the exultation of the divine light which streams into our spirit from the presence of the newborn Savior and transforms us from glory to glory in His image?

This is the mystery of light which shines upon us today and which the Church everywhere proclaims in her sacred chants and texts. *Tu lumen, tu splendor Patris* she sings at Lauds, not only addressing Him Who is before her mystically, but also pouring forth the light and splendor of God that radiates from Him within her own heart. This splendor does indeed shine in the heart of every one of us who has received Baptism, the sacrament of light. It shines more brightly in all of us who have been inebriated with the fire of the Holy Spirit, and blinded by the glorious light from the most blessed Body of the Savior Whom we have received as our mystical nourishment. Indeed, the chalice of salvation has come to us overflowing with divine fire and the Body of the Lord has burned away the darkness and impurity of worldliness that kept us from seeing the One Who dwells in the midst of us, and Whom we know not: "Our God is a consuming fire." Therefore, in her various orations, the Church prays in the following words: "O God, Who hast made this most holy night to shine forth with the brightness of the true light, grant we beseech Thee that we may enjoy His happiness in heaven, the mystery of whose light we have known on earth . . . Grant that we who are bathed in the new light of Thy Word made flesh, may show forth in our actions that which by faith shines in our minds . . . Grant of Thy bountiful grace that through this sacred communion in mystery (*haec sacrosancta commercia*), we may be found conformed to Him in whom our substance is united to Thee . . . May our gifts, we beseech Thee, O Lord, be agreeable to the mysteries of this day's Nativity, and ever pour down upon us peace: that even as He Who was born Man shone forth also as God, so these earthly fruits may bestow upon us that which is divine."

In all these prayers, the Church plunges us into the Light of God shining in the darkness of the world, in order that we may be illuminated and transformed by the presence of the newborn Savior, and thus that He may be born and truly live in us by making all our thoughts and actions light in Himself. What joy, then, that He who dwells eternally in the inaccessible light and peace of the Father has left the throne of His glory and descended to be one of us! Or rather, without leaving the bosom of the Father, veiling the too brilliant light of His glory in the cloud of human nature, He who is enthroned above the cherubim takes up His abode among us in a poor manger. This Child whom the shepherds, dazzled by the brilliance of the angelic host, can scarcely see in the darkness of the cave lit by Joseph's lantern, this Child is (by His divinity) the Ancient of Days, the Creator and Judge of Heaven and earth, of Whom the prophet Daniel wrote: "I beheld till thrones were placed and the Ancient of Days sat, His garment was as white as snow, and the hair of His head like clean wool; His throne like flames of fire: the wheels of it like a burning fire. A swift stream of fire issued forth before Him: thousands of thousands ministered to Him and ten thousand times a hundred thousand stood before Him." This, is Daniel's vision of the divinity of the Word Who, in His human nature, lies here helpless in the dark. But the Son of Man, who is here born, is Himself the Word, consubstantial with the Father. To this only-begotten Son, Who is equal to the

Father in all things as God, but less than the Father in so far as He is man, all power is given by the Father. So, Daniel says again: "I beheld therefore in the vision of the night, and lo one like the Son of Man came with the clouds of heaven, and he came even to the Ancient of Days and they presented Him before Him, and He gave Him power and glory and a kingdom, and all peoples, tribes and tongues shall serve Him, His power is an everlasting power that shall not be taken away and His kingdom that shall not be destroyed." This, then, is the King promised from the beginning of the world and of whose Kingdom there shall be no end.

Do not be afraid of Him. God has emptied Himself and come to us as a child, in order that we who have not been saved by fear, but only destroyed by it, may now take heart and be saved by confidence. In "emptying Himself" and taking the form of a servant the Lord laid aside His majesty and His divine power, in order to dwell among us in goodness and mercy. Hear what the Fathers say: "The power of God had appeared before in the creation of the world, and His wisdom in the government of that which He had created: but the kindness of His mercy now appears most clearly of all in His humanity. He had made Himself known to the Jews in signs and wonders . . . But the Jews were crushed by His power and the philosophers who sought impudently to penetrate secrets of His majesty were blinded by His glory." These are the words of Saint Bernard. Neither power nor glory, then, can save us: for if the power and glory of God reveal themselves to our naked eye we will be blinded by their light and consumed by their fire. What then can be done? Saint Bernard cries, as the Church too cries out from age to age: "Let Thy goodness then appear, O Lord, that man, Who is created in Thy image, may be conformed to it." *Appareat Domine bonitas, cui possit homo qui ad imaginem tuam creatus est, conformari.*

We have seen that God has indeed answered this prayer, for all His goodness, all His love and all His mercy (which we were unable to see in the fearful storm upon Sinai or in the desert whirlwind), all the gentleness of the great God has appeared to us in Christ. *Apparuit benignitas et humanitas salvatoris nostri Dei!*

The Child that lies in the manger, helpless and abandoned to the love of His creatures, dependent entirely upon them to be fed, clothed and sustained, remains the Creator and Ruler of the universe. Yet, in this human nature of His, He wills to be helpless that we may take Him into our care. For here is no mere matter of appearances. The poverty of the Child and of His mother, their loneliness and dereliction at Bethlehem, their need for food and clothing and support, these are all as real as our own needs and our own limitations. And why? Above all, because of the reality of His love. He has embraced our poverty and our sorrow out of love for us, in order to give us His riches and His joy. He has become as poor as the poorest of us, that no man may be held back from Him by false shame. For, the love with which this divine Child loves us is truly the love of a man-child, but also, and just as truly, the love of our Savior and

of our God. The arms with which He embraces us are
not strong enough to harm any man, though they are
the arms of God. What could be more evident than
that God, Who loves us, and Who hates nothing that
He has made, does not desire to hurt us? Can God
will anything but our good? No, it is we who plunge
to our own destruction by flying from His love.

Let us then, in the words of the Apostle, "deny
ungodliness and worldly desires and live soberly,
justly and godly in this world, looking for the blessed
hope and coming of the great God and our Savior,
Jesus Christ: Who gave Himself for us that He might
redeem us from all iniquity and might cleanse to
Himself a people acceptable, a pursuer of good
works." But Saint Paul speaks here of another coming
of the Lord, at the Last Judgment: for the Church
would have us remember that without the consummation of Christ's work on earth, its beginning would
have no meaning. The sacred Body which the Savior
of the world took to Himself in the womb of the
Virgin Mother has risen from death and reigns over
heaven and earth, enthroned at the right hand of the
Father. The Child whom we contemplate in mystery
this day lives in fact in the bosom of the Father where
He is ever begotten anew in the "day" of eternity,
and where He governs the course of the world and of
men's lives with omnipotent mercy. He Who is at
once a Child and a King, and an Infant, and the
Ancient of Days, looks with calm eyes upon the future day in which He shall give our flesh its share in
His final victory over death. In that day, He who was
once born to earth and time in a mortal Body will

clothe our mortality with incorruption. "The trumpet shall sound and the dead shall rise again incorruptible and we shall be changed." For God became man in order that men might become gods.

If we wish to see Christ in His glory, we must recognize Him now in His humility. If we wish His light to shine on our darkness and His immortality to clothe our mortality, we must suffer with Him on earth in order to be crowned with Him in Paradise. If we desire His love to transform us from glory to glory into His perfect likeness, we must love one another as He has loved us, and we must take our places at that blessed table where He Himself becomes our food, setting before us the Living Bread, the Manna which is sent to us from heaven, this day, to be the Life of the World.

Jesus, Who has come to nourish our spirit with His own Body and Blood, does so not to be transformed into us, but in order to transform us into Himself. He has given Himself to us in order that we may belong to Him. For the center of this great mystery is the Eternal Father's design to reestablish all things in Christ. This, says Saint Paul, is the "Mystery of His will . . . in the dispensation of the fullness of times, to reestablish all things in Christ, that are in heaven and on earth."

This Child and Redeemer Who comes amid the songs of angels to answer the prayers of all the Patriarchs and Prophets, and to satisfy the unrecognized longings of the whole lineage of Adam, exiled from Paradise, comes also to quiet the groanings of all creation. For, the whole world has been in labor and in mourning since the fall of man. The whole created universe, with all its manifold beauty and splendor, has travailed in disorder longing for the birth of a Savior. Every creature groaneth and travaileth in pain even until now . . . for the expectation of the creature waiteth for the revelation of the sons of God."

The Patriarchs and Prophets prayed for the coming of Christ in Bethlehem, and this first coming did not silence the groanings of creation. For, according to the words of the Apostle, which we have just heard, while man waited for the birth of Jesus in Judaea, the rest of the universe still waits for the revelation of Christ in His Church.

The mystery of Christmas therefore lays upon us all a debt and an obligation to the rest of men and to the whole created universe. We who have seen the light of Christ are obliged, by the greatness of the grace that has been given us, to make known the presence of the Savior to the ends of the earth. This we will do not only by preaching the glad tidings of His coming, but above all by revealing Him in our lives. Christ is born to us today, in order that He may appear to the whole world through us. This one day is the day of His birth, but every day of our mortal lives must be His manifestation, His divine Epiphany, in the world which He has created and redeemed.

[1956]

5

A HOMILY ON LIGHT
AND THE VIRGIN MARY

*"No man lights a lamp and puts it under a bushel
basket."* Matthew 5:15

God our Father and Creator, Who is pure being, pure
truth, pure light, in Whom there is no darkness,
willed to kindle the light of His truth outside Himself and for this reason He made the universe.

The first of His material creatures was light, the
purest and most beautiful of all visible beings, from
which comes the beauty and the visibility of all other
material creatures. Light was a material image of His
own truth and beauty. Yet it was only the beginning
of the work of God. It was not yet the pure light of
God Himself, shining mysteriously in a created being: it was only so to speak a shadow of God's light.

God, Who wished to kindle the lamp of His own
truth, fashioned the whole material creation as a
lampstand for the true light. We must always remember that matter is not a bushel basket under
which the light of God is hidden. Matter is dark as
long as it is without light: but it is not in itself a
principle of darkness. It is capable of receiving light

and truth in itself, and it can help to manifest them. Matter is dark only to those who seek no other light than matter itself. For them it is a source of darkness and of error. Now God made the lampstand, or the universe, by a word, commanding it to exist. But the lamp, man, He fashioned tenderly and carefully with His own hands.

As He made the lamp, He also breathed into it and kindled it with the light of His own truth, beauty and grace. For man, made in the image and likeness of God, shone with the very light of God within himself, he came into existence with divine light dwelling in his inmost being.

But as soon as the lamp was set on the lampstand, by an act of its own perverse choice, the lamp put out the light and refused to be rekindled.

Then there was a great darkness, even though the sun, moon and stars were all still shining where God had put them.

In the darkness, God continued patiently to prepare His true light: but now there was something in the lamp that had to be refashioned.

The lights which God kindled in the old Law were preparations for the perfect rekindling of the lamp: lights which were lit in worship and in justice, whenever man met God in liturgy, or in His works of mercy, justice and truth.

At first these lights were mysterious and quickly vanishing symbols like the rainbow shown in the covenant with Noah. Or they were frightening and inscrutable signs like the oven and torch shown in the covenant with Abraham:

When the sun had gone down and it was dark, behold, a smoking oven and a flaming torch passed between the pieces. On that day the Lord made a covenant with Abram, saying, "To your descendants I give this land, from the river of Egypt to the great river, the river Euphrates."

(Genesis 15:17–18)

Then at Sinai Yahweh set the whole mountain alight with a roaring fire hidden in cloud and thunder, which terrified the people:

Now when all the people perceived the thunderings and the lightnings and the sound of the trumpet and the mountain smoking, the people were afraid and trembled; and they stood afar off, and said to Moses, "You speak to us, and we will hear; but let not God speak to us, lest we die." And Moses said to the people, "Do not fear; for God has come to prove you, and that the fear of him may be before your eyes, that you may not sin." And the people stood afar off, while Moses drew near to the thick cloud where God was.

(Exodus 20:18–21)

And so it was seen that the light which God willed to kindle in man was too terrifying. Each time God approached the lamp, to light it again, the lamp was appalled and feared it would be destroyed. It fled from Him and hid in darkness. Then the Holy Spirit revealed a way of worship in which there were to be sacred lamps and lights, which would not terrify men but would yet speak to them gently of God's light. The lamps in the tabernacle were to be fed with "virgin oil," which would signify that virginal purity

of heart which awaits the Bridegroom in the silence
of night. (Leviticus 24:1–4)

For the lamps of virgin oil, the inspired craftsman,
the sacred artist Besalel made a lampstand, and perhaps he did not know, as he made it, that the Spirit in
him was secretly refashioning an image of the universe, a cosmic paradise tree, in which man, under the
form of innocent lamps, would shine again, full of the
light of God, but as yet only in figure.

It is a curious thing that perhaps all man's work has
in it something of this inescapable obsession—the
desire to create a paradise around man, the desire to
return to the beginning or to push on to an ideal
consummation.

The lampstand was made of pure beaten gold. The
base and the shaft of the lampstand were made of ham-
mered work; its cups, its capitals, and its flowers were
of one piece with it. And there were six branches going
out of its sides, three branches of the lampstand out
of one side of it and three branches of the lampstand out
of the other side of it; three cups made like almonds,
each with capital and flower, on one branch, and three
cups made like almonds, each with capital and flower
on the other branch—so for the six branches going out
of the lampstand.

(Exodus 37:17–19)

These are significant words: for they tell us a truth
about man's relation with the universe, and they
instruct us about the importance of man's work as he
lives in the world. Man, made in God's image, is
placed in the paradise of the world, a world which is

still paradise, but which man has lost, by becoming
alienated from himself and from the Creator.

In this world from which he is alienated, man can
come to find himself and recover his right relation to
the world and to God, by the work which God has
given him to do. Man's worship, his liturgy, should
rightly be not only worship but a theology of life, a
theology of work, planting in man the seeds of understanding and wisdom which will flower in his work.
But this means that man's work must be purified of
titanism, of self-will, of aspirations to self-assertion
and power. And this means that it must be delivered
from obsession with what man is not, with his past
and future, what he has ceased to be and has not yet
become, and is based on what man is in his present
reality. For only in the present can man come in full
contact with the truth willed for him and in him by
God. Thus creation will become once again a lampstand, and man the lamp will be placed on it in order
to be lit with the light of truth. For this is the light
which God really intends to kindle in us. When we
are in communion with other men and with the
cosmos by our will, the light of truth is kindled in us.

The Book of Proverbs says: "The light of Yahweh
is the spirit of man, penetrating to the depths of his
being." (Proverbs 20:27)

When the spirit of a holy man is illuminated with
the law of Yahweh, then the man himself becomes a
light to his fellow man. So the prophets were lamps
with which God "searched Jerusalem." David was
said to be the "Lamp of Israel." (II Samuel 21:17)

On the one hand, when Yahweh wills to manifest

Himself in His alienated creation, He does so in cloud, lightning and storm:

He bowed the heavens, and came down; thick darkness was under his feet. He rode on a cherub, and flew; he was seen upon the wings of the wind. He made darkness around him his canopy, thick clouds, a gathering of water. Out of the brightness before him coals of fire flamed forth. The Lord thundered from heaven, and the Most High uttered his voice. And he sent out arrows, and scattered them; lightning, and routed them. When the channels of the sea were seen, the foundations of the world were laid bare, at the rebuke of the Lord, at the blast of the breath of his nostrils.

(II Samuel 22:10–16)

Yet at the same time, while the storm rages outside in the world, the man who knows and trusts Yahweh, who sticks close to the Law of the Lord, perceives the Lord within himself as a lamp and a light to his feet:

For thou art my lamp, O Lord, and my God lightens my darkness . . . God is my strong refuge, He makes my way blameless.

(Id. 29, 33)

This text is familiar in the liturgy, where the Church applies it to Mary.

The Church celebrates, in Mary, the perfect rekindling of the pure light which had been extinguished by the sin of Adam. In Mary, the lamp was once more perfectly clean, burning with pure light, standing on the lampstand, illuminating the whole house of God, restoring meaning to all God's creatures, and showing the rest of men the way to return to the light: not that Mary was filled with any light of her own but because she was the first fruit of redemption, perfectly sanctified by the sacrifice of our redemption even before it was consummated, to give greater glory to the power of that sacrifice, and to prepare a way for the Lamb of God, the Light of the world, who was to come into the world through her consent and her obedience.

The liturgy applies to Mary the sublime texts from the Sapiential books about God's Wisdom itself. Since there is in Mary "nothing defiled," who is the "brightness of the eternal light and a mirror without stain. She is more beautiful than the sun, and compared with the light, she is found to be more pure than light itself."

How can these things be said of Mary? She is only a creature, and these words belong to the uncreated wisdom itself. But we must remember that the light that shines in Mary, the light that shone in Adam before his sin, and that God wished to shine in every man, is precisely the light of God's own wisdom, the reflection of His own truth, indeed His truth itself. For by the supreme liberality of God and the pure gift of His grace, man shares in the life, the light, the truth, the beauty of God and thus becomes the son of God in Christ.

No one has ever more perfectly contained the light of God than Mary who by the perfection of her purity and humility is, as it were, completely identified with truth like the clean window pane which vanishes entirely into the light which it transmits.

Mary is also described in the liturgy as the woman of the Apocalypse, "clothed with the sun with the

moon beneath her feet, and with a crown of twelve
stars about her head."

She is therefore filled with the light of the transfigured Christ, according to the words of the Gospel:
her garments are "white as snow and her face is like
the sun."

Thus she is "all beautiful," she is the "glory of
Jerusalem and the joy of Israel." Indeed, the light
that shines in Mary is the same light that is to shine in
the whole Church and in the entire cosmos recapitu-
lated in Christ. So, Mary is compared with the heavenly Jerusalem: "The Lord has shown us the heavenly Jerusalem filled with the light of God, and her
light is like crystal and precious stone."

We who are sinners need the protection and light
which comes from God. Without grace we cannot
know the true light. Without His light we will go
astray, and we will follow the false lights that our sin
has kindled in the world. For as the Book of Proverbs
tells us: "The light of the wicked is sin." (Proverbs
21:4)

Indeed, the world is hypnotized by strange and
terrible lights, the fires that proceed from the mouth
of Leviathan:

His sneezings flash forth light, and his eyes are like
the eyelids of the dawn. Out of his mouth go flaming
torches; sparks of fire leap forth. Out of his nostrils
comes forth smoke, as from a boiling pot and burning
rushes. His breath kindles coals, and a flame comes forth
from his mouth. In his neck abides strength, and terror
dances before him.

(Job 41:9–13)

This suggests to us the condition of our modern world in which, as Maritain has said, the great danger to society is the weakening of the sense of truth. The light that bursts from the mouth of Leviathan is not the light of truth but the flame of man's blind will to power.

For man today has lost consciousness of his need for truth. What he seeks is power. Truth is made to serve the ends of power. Truth is of no value unless it is expedient. When truth is not expedient, then it is deliberately manipulated and twisted to serve the aims of the powerful. Objective truth is considered irrelevant. It is derided by the powerful, who can change truth to suit themselves, and bend it this way and that for the sake of ambition and fortune.

It is a common trait of all the powerful materialist societies, that they are not so much interested in truth as in the creation and propagation of slogans and images. They specialize in thought-clichés, in glib formulas which made thought itself seem irrelevant. For to the man of power, thought is not expedient, especially in the subject whom he rules. What matters is will. Where power is primary, truth is made to bend to will. The will to power does not obey truth but manufactures its own truth, to suit policy and expediency. It imposes this fabrication ready-made on the subject to keep him from thinking for himself.

In such a condition, persons themselves become subservient to things. Indeed persons are treated as things. They are bought and sold like commodities. And therefore the rule of greed and fear replaces the rule of reason. Thought is regarded as a waste of time: all that matters is action for its own sake, action without reason and without ultimate purpose other than power.

But when power becomes more important than truth, when the affirmation of will becomes an end in itself to which all else is subordinated, then the whole purpose of the created universe is subverted and frustrated. The basic pattern of creation is this: material beings exist for man, and man exists for the glory of God. Created things stand as obstacles between man and God only when man himself is an obstacle, when his will has darkened the light of truth. But where the light of truth shines in man, and where he lives and acts according to that light, then all things find their proper place in relation to God by virtue of man's right use of them. They are sanctified and offered to God by man's creative work.

Thus everything else that has been created (except the angels) depends on man who is in the universe as the eye and the mind are in the body. If the eye is "single" or "simple," that is to say if it is pure, direct and true in its vision, then the whole body is full of light.

It follows then that the whole universe is in light or in darkness, spiritually, in proportion as man himself is in light or in darkness. If man's eye is "lightsome" with the spiritual beauty of grace, wisdom, understanding and divine sonship, then light will pass through him to pervade and transfigure the whole of creation: not of course by a kind of magical osmosis, but by the creative work of man's own spirit, a work born out of love for God the Creator and for our fellow man. Work that springs from this creative love is patterned on the truth implanted in our very being, by nature, and in our redeemed spirit by the Pneuma who is given us by the Risen Christ.

Man's obsession with power darkens and defiles the whole universe because it causes him to redefine all truth in terms of the power-struggle and to see all things in a partial, interested and fragmentary fashion. To define being in terms of power and will is to subject it to division and ultimately to atomize it. The uncontrolled obsession with will and appetite so divides and diminishes man that he cannot be whole, cannot be sane, and can never be at rest. But then he misuses and perverts everything he touches, and in the end all creation defies and frustrates him even while it obeys his supreme power.

As long as man seeks only to control the universe, he inevitably regards himself merely as a fragment of it. But the mystery of faith shows us he is indeed much more.

Man is more than a mere cog in a cosmic machine. Each person is in a way the end of the whole material creation which he transcends by his spiritual nature and by his vocation as a son of God. St Thomas was saying this when he said that all the value of the natural world was less than the value of one degree of grace in the soul of redeemed man. He was also saying this when he declared that the rational soul of man is the last end intended for all lesser natures.

Only in Mary is this vocation perfectly realized. This explains why the liturgy shows her identified with the creative wisdom of God, as if she were so to speak what He intended before all else when He planned and fashioned the mountains, the stars and the oceans of the world.

When He established the heavens I was there, when He marked out the vault over the face of the deep; when He made firm the skies above, when He fixed fast the foundations of the earth; when He set for the sea its limit, so that the waters should not transgress His command; then I was beside Him as His craftsman, and I was His delight day by day, playing before Him all the while, playing on the surface of the earth (and I found delight in the sons of men)."

(Proverbs 8:27–31)

In Mary is perfectly realized God's whole creative and redemptive plan. That is why she is said to be for us a light of truth and a pattern of life. That is why her spiritual beauty includes in itself all the beauty which we see here and there, in partial and incomplete form, in the universe. In her is all the beauty of the world, transfigured and elevated to a level beyond our comprehension: and yet since that perfection was reached by the fulfillment of the obediential potency in her nature, which is also our nature, there is a certain connaturality in us which makes us respond to her transcendent radiance even though it remains obscure to us. We cannot help but see that she is, like ourselves, a human creature whose littleness has been glorified in the light of Christ and who has been saved from the power of darkness and evil by the grace of His Cross.

It remains then for us to celebrate her immaculate beauty, to open our hearts to the same light of truth which sanctified her, the same grace which made her pleasing to the Most High, Who is her creator as He is ours, and who wishes to see realized in us the same ineffable mystery of light. More than that, He wishes to see the whole world saved and transfigured in that light, by reason of our perfect acceptance of His gift, His love and His grace and our transmission of the power of His love to all men and to all other beings by our work, our prayer and our love.

[1962]

6

THE NAME OF THE LORD

The author of the Epistle to the Hebrews opens his testimony concerning the High Priesthood of the Incarnate Word by contrasting God's revelation of Himself to men "through the ministry of angels" and His manifestation of Himself in His Son. The very first words of the Epistle recall the fact that "in old days God spoke to our fathers in many ways and by many means, through the prophets." But now He has spoken in a Son who inherits the universe which is also created in Him. (Cf. Colossians 1:16). He is the image of the Father's glory, sitting at the Father's right hand in majesty "superior to the angels as He has inherited a name Superior to theirs." (Hebrews 1: 1–5). Perhaps the writer of Hebrews also had in mind the contrast that is found in the Torah between the appearances of the mysterious "malakh' Yahweh" (the angel of the Lord), and the Lord's much more pure, more immediate and more direct revelation of Himself in *His Name,* Yahweh.

As a matter of fact, in the Torah the experience of seeing, or perhaps even wrestling with the "angel of the Lord" (Genesis 32:24 f) was reserved for very special individuals, and besides it had something in common with the religious experiences of the other peoples of the near East. (Cf. Judges 13:3–16).

The angel, however, refuses to reveal his name. He remains an anonymous manifestation of divine power in an extraordinary experience which breaks in upon the life of an individual and leaves him permanently changed. (Genesis 32:25) In contrast with the vision of the Lord through His angel, is a personal confrontation with Him in and through His Name. Note however that in Exodus 23:21 the Lord tells Moses that His angel will precede Israel, *"and my Name is in him."* Here the Name of the Lord is evidently transcendent and divine, while the angel remains a created being, in and through whom the Name of the Lord is manifested by His action in saving His People.

Yet the experience of knowing and invoking the Name of Yahweh was nothing esoteric, since it was given to all the members of the holy People. Indeed, that was one of the things that made it a people, and holy. Knowing the Lord's Name, they were *His* people. His Name dwelt among them, and was invoked upon them, and was known in their midst. (Exodus 23:21; Deuteronomy 12:5; I Kings 8:16–30; Numbers 6:22–27.) Yet at the same time, the knowledge of the Name of the Lord definitely and clearly separated everyone who received it, from the multifarious nature cults and kingship cults of the "nations." He who "knew the Name" of Yahweh, by that fact knew the nothingness of all other gods, and was bound to "hallow" or "sanctify" the Name of Yahweh by a total obedience, fidelity and dedication that abjured any division of heart and any temptation to share the cult of Yahweh with that of another. (Cf. Leviticus 18:21.) Any attempt to worship another god, together with Yahweh was not only a violation of the first and most important commandment, but it also "profaned the Name of Yahweh."

That God should reveal His Name to His people was the most important of all gifts, the gift which contained in itself every other gift. To bestow knowledge of His Name, was at the same time to grant His people power to enter into His presence, to invoke him, to commune with Him, to praise Him, and to find, in the liturgical sanctification ("hallowing") of His Name, the central meaning of their own existence as His people. This was therefore something more than the revelation of knowledge "about" Himself, or even a revelation of His essence. It is a revelation of His Presence as a transcendent, personal and existential fact, indeed as the supreme actuality. And hence the Name Yahweh, even more than the other Names of God, is expressive of the divine majesty. By His Name, Yahweh would be personally present wherever He was invoked in a manner that accorded with His will, and therefore manifested fidelity to the true meaning of His Name. (Cf. John 14:13–14).

He would grant His People the capacity to "remember" His Name in a cult especially established by Him for this purpose. This "remembering" of the Name of Yahweh was, of course, more than a mere recalling to conscious awareness: it implied a personal confrontation in worship and the renewal of covenant obedience. (Joshua 24:14–25).

The revelation of the Name Yahweh was at the same time more and less than the revelation of the Divine Essence and Attributes. More because it made God present in His personal being, in all the immediacy and urgency of a gratuitous, redemptive love. Less, because it did not give detailed knowledge of His nature.

On the other hand, the Name El-Elohim - Allah tends to be more a revelation of the divine nature, the divine power. But this is simply the common semitic name for God and is not a special revelation of Yahweh to His people. In fact, "El" can designate *any* God, and there are many points in common between El-Shaddai (God Almighty) in the Old Testament with the "High God" of the Canaanites (cf. Genesis 35:9–15.) El-Elohim is the all-powerful creator and Lord of Nature, who manifests Himself in cosmic theophanies. Yahweh is the Lord of the "salvation-history" of the chosen People, who reveals not only His power but His unfailing mercy (*chesed*) and His fidelity (*emet*).

To remember the Name of Yahweh was to enter into His presence in and through the all holy Name as it was invoked by the sacred assembly: but this was not merely a question of collective religious awe at the transcendent power of the divine nature, El-Shaddai, El-Elohim. It was also and above all an awareness of being in the presence of the *Person* of the Lord, Yahweh, and consequently it meant awareness of, submission to the expression of His free and personal

will to glorify His Name in the midst of His people,
by the saving power of His *chesed,* or unfailing love.

Even where the Lord manifested Himself, in pre-
Mosaic times, through an angel, there was felt an
immediate need to seek the "name" of the "man of
God" who had thus appeared. Manoah, for instance,
wants to offer sacrifice to the angel who has promised
him the birth of a son, Samson. The angel tells him to
offer sacrifice to the Lord instead. Manoah, still not
comprehending the full meaning of this situation,
asks: "What is your name that we may honor you
when your words come true?" The angel of the Lord
answered him: "Why do you ask my name, which is
mysterious?" Then Manoah took the kid with a cereal
offering and offered it on a rock to the Lord "whose
works are mysterious." (Judges 13:18–19. Note the
following verses, to the end of the Chapter. Cf. Genesis 32; 30.)

Here in this curious text which, doubtless, reflects
the confluence of a variety of primitive religious
traditions, and is therefore somewhat ambiguous, we
see the importance primitive men attached to the
knowledge of the *Name* of any supernatural being,
who might be invoked as a helper or intercessor. To
call upon the Name of such a one was to enter into
contact with a power greater than man's, and to know
the name of that power was, in some sense, to be-
friend it. The life and power of an intelligent being
(in the African Bantu sense of *muntu*) is mysteriously present in his name. In the case of human or
angelic beings, the name exercises a power over the
person himself—if he is called, he cannot help re-

sponding in some way. Yahweh can of course refuse to hear when His name is invoked, but He freely commits Himself by a promise to hear and respond when His Name is invoked by His people in the sacred assembly, or even by the faithful individual:

Because he cleaves to me in love, I will deliver him;
I will protect him because he knows my name.
When he calls to me, I will answer him;
I will be with him in trouble,
I will rescue him and honor him.
With long life I will satisfy him, and show him
my salvation.
(Ps. 90/91/:14–16 RSV)
(cf. Ps. 9:11; 39/40/:5, etc.)

As for Yahweh Himself, His "name shared directly in His own holiness and was, so to speak, the double of His being."[1] Hence, to remember His Name was to enter into the presence of His awful majesty. Not only that, the Name of Yahweh was actually the "embodiment of saving revelation."[2] To remember the Name of Yahweh was to remember all His merciful and faithful promises, all His interventions in history. In a certain sense, the past, present and future came together in the invocation of the divine Name. The realization of past promises, in the saving history of the People of God merged with the hope that present needs would be met with the same unfailing fidelity and mercy as in the glorious past. In this hope they were already so to speak realized.

[1] C. Von Rad. Old Testament Theology, New York, 1962, Vol. 1, p. 183.
[2] *Ibid.*, p. 186.

Thus the invocation of the Name of Yahweh in time, in the cult, and in history, implied the discovery of a dynamism in the experience of the people of God which, in later times, would take on an eschatological orientation. Thus the "sanctifications" of the Name of the Lord brought together the beginning and the end, the creation and the final judgement, and foreshadowed the establishment of the promised eschatological kingdom. In the New Testament Apocalypse, the Lord, Kurios, would declare Himself to be "the Alpha and Omega, the beginning and the end."

The primitive revelation of the Name of Yahweh at Horeb was still far from this. Nevertheless, the Name and Presence of Yahweh would remain at once the dynamic center of the life and history of God's people, and it would also theologically "take the place which in other cults was occupied by the cultic image."[3]

Yahweh was truly a "living God" because He was present, not in a dead image but in a powerful and dynamic personal presence, His Name which "dwelt in the midst of His people."

If the revelation of the Name of Yahweh had been merely the revelation of the divine nature or essence, it might in some way have become accessible to the other nations. They might have deduced it from observing nature created by Him. It might have become part of their cultic heritage and merged with their syncretistic worship built around the season

3 *Ibid.,* p. 183.

cycle and the creative forces of natural life. After all, this would only have meant linking up a cosmic worship with a supreme metaphysical source, the divine nature of the Ruler of the Universe. But the revelation of the Name of Yahweh was far more than that. It was the revelation of a personal freedom intervening, with His own wise and inscrutable purposes, in the history of His own elect people. Consequently the meaning of His intervention was not accessible, and could not be accessible, to anyone who was not involved in the salvific plan of Yahweh.

The Israelite who sooner or later yielded to the temptation to identify Yahweh, more or less in good faith, with the Baalim, was in fact forgetting the purely personal character of the free, deliberate self-revelation of God in His Name. He was reverting to the concept of a divine nature: a concept which was less demanding because, precisely, it did not insist upon so serious and so earnest confrontation of hearts and wills, and hence required, instead of personal and particular obedience, only a kind of general submission to the forces implanted in nature by a divine creative, or perhaps only directive, power. The various Baals, of course, all had their proper names. But to invoke them was to invoke a *force,* and not a free and personal presence filled with the power to judge and to have mercy. A force, indeed, which might be unpredictable in its action: hence not subject to what we would call "scientific" control. Yet this unpredictability sprang not from personal freedom but from the capriciousness of a cosmic force which eludes conscious control.

The primitive revelation of the Name of Yahweh was not the revelation of a name like any other. YHWH, the "unspeakable tetragrammaton" (Origen), is in some sense not a name at all. Some scholars interpret Exodus 3:14 as a *refusal* of Yahweh to manifest His Name and identity, a rebuff to an impertinent question! This is hardly likely, when Moses is the one entrusted with the revelation of Yahweh and His plan of salvation to the chosen People. Yet there is no question that the statement "I am who I am" is in some sense evasive. In effect, Yahweh is refusing to declare or define His ineffable Nature, but is clearly and forcefully manifesting *His presence and His being as a Person* with a free and salvific plan emanating from an abyss of incomprehensible and loving mercy (cf. Exodus 34:6).

On the other hand it is certain that the form YHWH, which no one knows with certainty how to pronounce, was introduced in late Old Testament times to ensure that the Holy Name would never be treated with the slightest irreverence. Thus it ceased to be spoken at all. The Manual of Discipline of the Qumran community prescribes expulsion for a member who dared to pronounce the ineffable Name. When the Name of God was read aloud in the cult it was replaced by *Adonai* (Lord) and this was followed by the *Kyrios* of the Septuagint and the *Dominus* of the Vulgate.

Clement of Alexandria however said (*Stromateis* V.6.34), "The tetragram and mystic name which was grasped only by those to whom the impenetrable was accessible, is pronounced Ιαουε (Yahweh)."[4] A modern Biblical scholar writes: "As a primary religious feeling the name Yahweh called up the idea of the living, awe inspiring presence of God."[5] Hence we should be grateful to the editors of the *Bible de Jerusalem* for giving us the Name Yahweh everywhere instead of "Lord."

The Name Yahweh expresses the simplest, most direct and most powerful manifestation of God as *Person* in the Old Testament. The third chapter of Exodus is one of the most important texts in the Bible. It forms the basis not only for the Christian and Jewish theology, but also for the whole Religious concept of Islam. It is a text that must be known, meditated and absorbed by a believer in any one of these religions.

After the episode of the burning bush at Horeb (Exodus 3:1–12) where Moses is told that he must go and bring the Israelites out of Egypt, and that he must say he has been "sent" for this purpose, Moses understandably asks: "If they want to know who sent me, what Name shall I give them?" It is important that the "power" which offers himself for the salvation of Israel, should be identified: whether as the God of the Fathers, *or* Abraham, *or* of Isaac, *or* of Jacob (there might possibly be a choice), or as some other God. For instance He might simply be the God of this locality, Mount Horeb. The answer of Yahweh

---

[4] See the article of G. Lambert, S.J., "Que Signifie le Nom Divin YHWH," *Nouvelle Revue Theologique*, 1952, No. 9, p. 897 ff.
[5] Th. C. Vriezen, *An Outline of Old Testament Theology*, Oxford, 1960, p. 195.

meant, among other things, that He was not the God of some particular place or tribe or natural force. In effect, it is that he is not "one of the gods." Nor is He simply a nature among natures, a being among beings. The reply in Exodus 3:14 is certainly not a statement of "what kind of being" has sent Moses into Egypt. It is a declaration of the personal and transcendent presence of the invisible one who now speaks to Moses and who will also be present with him in Egypt.

The precise meaning of this statement has considerably exercised recent scholarship. Linguistic studies have found various ways of deriving YHWH from different forms of the verb "to be." Traditionally, Catholic theology has given this a metaphysical interpretation, which is quite legitimate as a *development* of its revealed content. It is however not altogether clear that the primitive meaning of the statement corresponds exactly to the rather special implications of the *Septuagint* (*eimi ho on*) and the Vulgate (*Ego sum qui sum*). In these versions there is a plausible and legitimate emphasis on the declaration of the absolute aseity of God: God *is* in Himself, depending on no other being, exalted above all beings, not to be confused with any, pure being, pure act, existing purely *a se*. The Vulgate can suggest two interpretations: I am who am, in the sense of I am *He who Is*. Or, more cryptically and concretely, I am *who I am* with the implication that God thus reveals *that* He is but not *who or what He is*.

Doubtless there is in this revelation of the divine being a clear implication of aseity, infinite reality, pure actuality and eternity. God is He who is, and in contrast to His pure being, all transient things "are not." Above all, the other beings which claim to be gods are simply delusions.

Other interesting possibilities have been advanced by modern scholarship and all of them tend to be, as we would say, more "existential" than those we have just discussed.

"I am He who *causes to be*." This also could be implicitly contained in the traditional Catholic elucidation of the Septuagint and Vulgate texts.

"I am what I will be." A more dynamic, less static, extrapolation of "I am what I am." *"I will be what I will be."* This is more mysterious, and the emphasis is more dynamic still. It declares the infinite freedom of Yahweh, while at the same time focussing our attention not on His being but on His activity, since in this interpretation there seems to be an implication of what Yahweh will *be to Israel,* that is, by what acts of mercy or judgement He intends, inscrutably, to manifest Himself in Israel, and be present in the midst of Israel.

Similar to this is another interpretation which is very attractive, "I am the *one who loves passionately*." This rests on a linguistic hypothesis which need not detain us here. Finally, Von Rad inclines to the most satisfactory interpretation in the light of present scripture studies: "I am the one Present," or perhaps "I am the one who will be present (when the crisis takes place in Egypt)."

This accords with the context, Exodus 3:12, in which the Lord says, in sending Moses to Egypt "I will be with you." But it is not redundant. Yahweh is saying that He *will be* present because He is the one who *is* present. Not that His presence is a metaphysical necessity, but a religious and transcendent fact of a quite unique character. Moses is aware of the altogether extraordinary and gratuitous reality of God's presence to him here at Horeb. This in itself constitutes and implies a promise of that same presence and powerful protection in the future. Thus the reality of Yahweh's presence is perceived not by a metaphysical intuition but by theological faith and hope and therefore it belongs not to the philosophical order, is not an awareness of *nature,* but a *personal relationship* of a supremely religious kind.

Buber brings this out in his translation: "I will be there as the *I* that will be there."

If at first sight this choice of possible interpretations seems confusing, we need not waste time trying to select one alone, to the exclusion of all the others. They are all good possibilities and hence the best thing for the average reader of the Bible to do is to take them all into account, and see them as complementary aspects of a hidden content which doubtless far exceeds them all. The very fact of these different interpretations, in their differences and in their common elements, points to an extremely clear and powerful primitive revelation of God, an experience which in its existential and spiritual impact goes beyond any other recorded in any document to which we have access, apart from the radically different revelations of God's presence and action in the New Testament. What marks this revelation out from all other records of God's manifestation of Himself to men is its special character as *personal, existential and free.*

It is in no sense a deduction from a natural experience. It is not an awareness of transcendent unity, arrived at through mystical liberation. It is even beyond what can be described, in Buber's famous term, as an "I-Thou" relationship. It is the presence of Him who is present, in a "Name" that eludes metaphysical elaboration because it is the source, the root and in some sense the embodiment of theology. However, it is not simply the root *concept* from which a theological system grows. The Name Yahweh is the source of theology in the sense that it is the living center around which the tribes of Israel gather in that unity which will enable them all to "attend to his law" (Psalm 77:1) and learn His ways while celebrating the great works of His power and of His unfailing mercy. The Name Yahweh is the heart of a living theology because, when it is invoked, the light, strength, presence, mercy and peace of Yahweh are shed upon His people. In calling upon the Name of Yahweh, they *live* their theology, or rather theology lives and works in them.

It must not however be imagined that this is reducible to a complacently nationalistic "Gott mit uns" doctrine, a sure guarantee of collective euphoria, prosperity and pride!

The presence of Yahweh can mean blessing or punishment, mercy or destruction. The living and holy Name of the Lord dwells in the midst of His people as a terrible force for judgement. Far from lending His power to the People as a means to achieve their own shortsighted political ends, Yahweh glorifies His Name by refusing to let it be a quasi-magical means subservient to man's will. Indeed, to call upon the Name of Yahweh for one's own purely secular purpose is a profanation of His Name akin to magic. In that event, the Name of Yahweh will bring destruction upon His people, and in the cataclysm itself they "will know that I am Yahweh."

Because the land is full of bloody crimes and the city is full of violence, I will bring the worst of the nations to take possession of their houses; I will put an end to their proud might, and their holy places shall be profaned. When anguish comes, they will seek peace, but there shall be none. Disaster comes upon disaster, rumor follows rumor; they seek a vision from the prophet, but the law perishes from the priest, and counsel from the elders. The king mourns, the prince is wrapped in despair, and the hands of the people of the land are palsied by terror. According to their way I will do to them, and according to their own judgments I will judge them; *and they shall know that I am Yahweh.*

(Ezekiel 7:23–27)

You have feared the sword; and I will bring the sword upon you, says the Lord God. And I will bring you forth out of the midst of it, and give you into the hands of foreigners, and execute judgments upon you. You shall fall by the sword; I will judge you at the border of Israel; and you shall know that I am Yahweh. This city shall not be your caldron, nor shall you be the flesh in the midst of it; I will judge you at the border of Israel; and you shall know that I am Yahweh; for you have not walked in my statutes, nor executed

my ordinances, but have acted according to the ordinances of the nations that are round about you.
(Ezekiel 11:8–12)

Yet at the same time the infallibly faithful mercy of Yahweh will have the last word. Even though Israel may have defiled His Name among the Gentiles (Ezekiel 36:22, 23) He will renew His people and give them new life in His Spirit, making them a new people, and thus paradoxically His "Name will be magnified among the gentiles" by His mercy to the chosen ones whom He has chastened and then brought back to Himself.

Therefore say to the house of Israel, Thus says the Lord God: It is not for your sake, O house of Israel, that I am about to act, but for the sake of my holy name, which you have profaned among the nations to which you came. And I will vindicate the holiness of my great name, which has been profaned among the nations, and which you have profaned among them; and the nations will know that I am Yahweh, says the Lord God, when through you I vindicate my holiness before their eyes. For I will take you from the nations, and gather you from all the countries, and bring you into your own land. I will sprinkle clean water upon you, and you shall be clean from all your uncleannesses, and from all your idols I will cleanse you. A new heart I will give you, and a new spirit I will put within you; and I will take out of your flesh the heart of stone and give you a heart of flesh. And I will put my Spirit within you, and cause you to walk in my statutes and be careful to observe my ordinances. You shall dwell in the land which I gave to your fathers; and you shall be my

people, and I will be your God. And I will deliver you
from all your uncleannesses; and I will summon the
grain and make it abundant and lay no famine upon
you. I will make the fruit of the tree and the increase
of the field abundant, that you may never again suffer
the disgrace of famine among the nations. Then you
will remember your evil ways, and your deeds that were
not good; and you will loathe yourselves for your in-
iquities and your abominable deeds. It is not for your
sake that I will act, says the Lord God; let that be
known to you. Be ashamed and confounded for your
ways, O house of Israel.

(Ezekiel 36:22–32)

The theme of Yahweh's Name becoming known to
the gentiles and His praise resounding to the ends of
the earth is one of the chief messages of Deutero-Isaias
(Isaias 65:1; 56:1–7, 60; cf. Michaeas 4:1–5). Here we
begin to see the eschatological implications of the
Name of Yahweh which will be made known clearly
to His enemies, in judgment, after a period in which
it has no longer been invoked at all (Isaias 64:2, 7)
even in Israel. Then His Name will be "great among
the gentiles" (Malachy 1:11). In the magnificent 60th
chapter of Isaias, and in the Epiphany liturgy, we see
all the nations coming out of darkness to the radiant
light of Yahweh rising over Jerusalem. They are
drawn to her "because of the Name of Yahweh your
God and because of the holy one of Israel who has
glorified you" (Isaias 60:9). Yet this return of the
light of the divine name presupposes a period of
darkness, absence and silence, when even the People
of God seems not to be His People (Osee 1:9).

But in any case, it is for His Name's sake that Yahweh finally shows mercy (Isaias 48:9, 10), for only thus is He fully true to the promise implied in His original revelation of Himself as the ever present and ever faithful bestower of compassionate and redemptive love (hesed). Hence the Name of Yahweh once revealed, is a permanent promise of mercy and salvation, since in revealing His Being, and giving His Name to be invoked, Yahweh commits Himself in some sense to save a world in which His Name is present. And because the Name of Yahweh is present in the world even in silence, when He is "forgotten" by the majority of men, it remains as a dormant flame at once of judgment and of mercy, ready to flare out at the moment determined by His inscrutable and salvific designs. This culminating point of the salvation history, when the Name of the Lord will resound to the ends of the earth and will be greeted by the response of universal praise, the *alleluia* of the nations, is the *Day of the Lord,* the Day of Yahweh.

At first all the earth shall be silent before Him (Sophonias 1:7), then the "word of the Lord" shall descend upon all the nations (Sophonias 2:5, etc.) to judge and purify the world, confronting false prophets who invoke His name without obeying His truth, destroying all the false gods and the power of the worldly cities (Sophonias 3). But finally, "in the day of His resurrection" the Lord will enable all the nations to call upon Him in purity of worship and in true unity, built around the "remnant" of the poor, the *anawim,* remaining as a kind of nucleus of holi-

ness because they continued to trust in His Name
when all had forgotten Him.

> "Therefore wait for me," says Yahweh,
> "for the day when I arise as a witness.
> For my decision is to gather nations,
> to assemble kingdoms,
> to pour out upon them my indignations,
> all the heat of my anger;
> for in the fire of my jealous wrath
> all the earth shall be consumed.

> "Yea, at that time I will change the speech
>   of the peoples
> to a pure speech,
> that all of them may call on the name of
>   the Yahweh
> and serve him with one accord.
> From beyond the rivers of Ethiopia
> my suppliants, the daughter of my dispersed
>   ones,
> shall bring my offerings.

> "On that day you shall not be put to shame
> because of the deeds by which you have
>   rebelled against me;
> for then I will remove from your midst
> your proudly exultant ones,
> and you shall no longer be haughty
> in my holy mountain.
> For I will leave in the midst of you
> a people humble and lowly.
> They shall seek refuge in the name of
> Yahweh,
> those who are left in Israel;

they shall do no wrong
and utter no lies,
nor shall there be found in their mouth
a deceitful tongue.
For they shall pasture and lie down,
and none shall make them afraid."

(Sophonias 3:8–13)

You will take up this taunt against the king
of Babylon:

"How the oppressor has ceased,
the insolent fury ceased!
Yahweh has broken the staff of the wicked,
the scepter of rulers,
that smote the peoples in wrath
with unceasing blows,
that ruled the nations in anger
with unrelenting persecution . . ."

(Isaias 14:4–6)

It is not surprising to find these same themes taken up again in the Apocalypse, where trust in the Name of the Lord is what gives the martyrs strength to remain faithful in the last great tribulations (cf. Apocalypse 2:3, 13, etc.). At the same time, however, the persecution is let loose against them precisely because of the Lord's Name, *propter nomen meum* (John 15:21). Hence the fidelity of the martyrs is summed up in the expression "to hold fast to my Name" (Apocalypse 2:13; cf. 3:11). The victory of faith is rewarded by the Name of the Lord being written upon the victorious one, who becomes a pillar in the City of God (Apocalypse 3:12, 14:1). What is the "Name" that is thus invoked and honored in the visions of the New Testament Apocalypse? It is the Name which was given by Joseph to Mary's child, at the command of the angel (Matthew 1:21): Ye-shuah, *Yahweh saves,* or, in the form familiar to us: Jesus. Thus the Name which is said, in Hebrew, to be "inherited" by the Incarnate Word is the same "I am" revealed to Moses, present in the midst of the People of God throughout the Salvation history. That is why Jesus said, "Before Abraham was, *I am*" (John 8:58). The Christian faith then sees in the *Person* of Jesus the living, actual presence of the ineffable Name.

[1962]

7

ASH WEDNESDAY

Even the darkest moments of the liturgy are filled with joy, and Ash Wednesday, the beginning of the lenten fast, is a day of happiness, a Christian feast. It cannot be otherwise, as it forms part of the great Easter cycle.

The Paschal Mystery is above all the mystery of life, in which the Church, by celebrating the death and resurrection of Christ, enters into the Kingdom of Life which He has established once for all by His definitive victory over sin and death. We must remember the original meaning of Lent, as the *ver sacrum,* the Church's "holy spring" in which the catechumens were prepared for their baptism, and public penitents were made ready by penance for their restoration to the sacramental life in a communion with the rest of the Church. Lent is then not a season of punishment so much as one of healing. There is joy in the salutary fasting and abstinence of the Christian who eats and drinks less in order that his mind may be more clear and receptive to receive the sacred nourishment of God's word, which the whole Church announces and meditates upon in each day's liturgy throughout Lent. The whole life and teaching of Christ pass before us, and Lent is a season of special reflexion and prayer, a forty-day retreat in which each Christian, to the extent that he is able, tries to follow Christ into the desert by prayer and fasting.

Some, monks and ascetics, will give themselves especially to fasting and vigils, silence and solitude in these days, and they will meditate more deeply on the word of God. But all the faithful should listen to the word as it is announced in the liturgy or in Bible services and respond to it according to their ability. In this way, for the whole Church, Lent will not be merely a season simply of a few formalized penitential practices, half understood and undertaken without interest, but a time of *metanoia,* the turning of all minds and hearts to God in preparation for the celebration of the Paschal Mystery in which some will for the first time receive the light of Christ, others will be restored to the communion of the faithful, and all will renew their baptismal consecration of their lives to God, in Christ.

The cross of ashes, traced upon the forehead of each Christian, is not only a reminder of death but inevitably (though tacitly) a pledge of resurrection. The ashes of a Christian are no longer mere ashes. The body of a Christian is a temple of the Holy Ghost, and though it is fated to see death, it will return again to life in glory. The cross, with which the ashes are traced upon us, is the sign of Christ's victory over death. The words "Remember man that thou art dust, and that to dust thou shalt return" are not to be taken as the quasi-form of a kind of "sacrament of death" (as if such a thing were possible). It might be good stoicism to receive a mere reminder of our condemnation to die, but it is not Christianity. The declaration that the body must fall temporarily into dust is a challenge to spiritual combat, that our burial may be "in Christ" and that we may rise with Him to "live unto God."

The ashes of this Wednesday are not merely a sign of death, but a promise of life to those who do penance. And yet the ashes are clearly a summons to penance, fasting and compunction.

Hence the seemingly paradoxical character of the Ash Wednesday liturgy. The gospel charges us to avoid outward signs of grief and, when we fast, to anoint our heads and to wash our faces. Yet we receive a smear of ashes on our heads. There must be grief in this day of joy. It is a day, we shall see, in which joy and grief go together hand in hand: for that is the meaning of compunction—a sorrow which pierces, which liberates, which gives hope and therefore joy. Compunction is a baptism of sorrow, in which the tears of the penitent are a psychological but also deeply religious purification, preparing and disposing him for the sacramental waters of baptism or for the sacrament of penance. Such sorrow brings joy because it is at once a mature acknowledgment of guilt and the acceptance of its full consequences: hence it implies a religious and moral adjustment to reality, the acceptance of one's actual condition, and the acceptance of reality is always a liberation from the burden of illusion which we strive to justify by our errors and our sins. Compunction is a necessary sorrow, but it is followed by joy and relief because it wins for us one of the greatest blessings: the light of truth and the grace of humility. The tears of the Christian penitent are real tears, but they bring joy.

Only the inner rending, the tearing of the heart, brings this joy. It lets out our sins, and lets in the clean air of God's spring, the sunlight of the days that advance toward Easter. Rending of the garments lets in nothing but the cold. The rending of heart which is spoken of in the lesson from Joel is that "tearing away" from ourselves and our *vetustas*—the "oldness" of the old man, wearied with the boredom and drudgery of an indifferent existence, that we may turn to God and taste His mercy, in the liberty of His sons.

When we turn to Him, what do we find? That "He is gracious and merciful, patient and rich of mercy." He even speaks to us in His own words, saying: "Behold I will send you corn and wine and oil and you shall be filled with them: and I will no more make you a reproach among the nations." This at the beginning of a forty days' fast!

It is necessary that at the beginning of this fast, the Lord should show Himself to us in His mercy. The purpose of Lent is not only expiation, to satisfy the divine justice, but above all a preparation to rejoice in His love. And this preparation consists in receiving the gift of His mercy—a gift which we receive in so far as we open our hearts to it, casting out what cannot remain in the same room with mercy.

Now one of the things we must cast out first of all is

fear. Fear narrows the little entrance of our heart. It shrinks up our capacity to love. It freezes up our power to give ourselves. If we were terrified of God as an inexorable judge, we would not confidently await His mercy, or approach Him trustfully in prayer. Our peace, our joy in Lent are a guarantee of grace.

In laying upon us the light cross of ashes, the Church desires to take off our shoulders all other heavy burdens—the crushing load of worry and obsessive guilt, the dead weight of our own self-love. We should not take upon ourselves a "burden" of penance and stagger into Lent as if we were Atlas, carrying the whole world on his shoulders.

Perhaps there is small likelihood of our doing so. But in any case, penance is conceived by the Church less as a burden than as a liberation. It is only a burden to those who take it up unwillingly. Love makes it light and happy. And that is another reason why Ash Wednesday is filled with the lightness of love.

In some monastic communities, monks go up to receive the ashes barefoot. Going barefoot is a joyous thing. It is good to feel the floor or the earth under your feet. It is good when the whole church is silent, filled with the hush of men walking without shoes. One wonders why we wear such things as shoes anyway. Prayer is so much more meaningful without them. It would be good to take them off in church all the time. But perhaps this might appear quixotic to those who have forgotten such very elementary satisfactions. Someone might catch cold at the mere thought of it—so let's return to the liturgy.

To say there is joy in Ash Wednesday is not to empty the procession of its sorrows and anguish. "Save me O God," we cry at the very beginning, "for the waters are come in even unto my soul." This is not a song of joy. If we present our selves before God to receive ashes from the hand of the priest it is because we are convinced of our sinfulness.

That is a weak way of putting it. Sin is a thing that needs to be talked about in concrete and existential terms. A sinner, in the way the liturgy understands him, is not a man with a theoretical conviction that violation of the law brings punishment for guilt. A sinner is a drowning man, a sinking ship. The waters are bursting into him on all sides. He is falling apart under the pressure of the storm that has been breaking up his will, and now the waters rush into the hold and he is dragged down. They are closing over his head, and he cries out to God: "the waters are come in even unto my soul."

Ash Wednesday is for people who know what it means for their soul to be logged with these icy waters: all of us are such people, if only we can realize it.

There is confidence everywhere in Ash Wednesday, yet that does not mean unmixed and untroubled security. The confidence of the Christian is always a confidence in spite of darkness and risk, in the presence of peril, with every evidence of possible disaster. "Let us emend for the better in those things in which we have sinned through ignorance: lest suddenly overtaken by the day of death we seek space for repentance and are not able to find it."

The last words are sobering indeed. And note, it is the sins we have not been fully aware of that we must emend. Once again, Lent is not just a time for squaring conscious accounts: but for realizing what we had perhaps not seen before. The light of Lent is given us to help us with this realization.

Nevertheless, the liturgy of Ash Wednesday is not focussed on the sinfulness of the penitent but on the mercy of God. The question of sinfulness is raised precisely because this is a day of mercy, and the just do not need a Savior.

Nowhere will we find more tender expressions of the divine mercy than on this day. His mercy is kind. He looks upon us "according to the multitude of Thy tender mercies." In the introit we sing: "Thou hast mercy upon all (*Misereris omnium*), O Lord, and hatest none of the things which Thou hast made, overlooking the sins of men for the sake of repentance and sparing them, because Thou art the Lord our God."

How good are these words of Wisdom in a time when on all sides the Lord is thought by men to be a God who hates. Those who deny Him say they do so because evil in the world could be the work only of a God that hated the world.

But even those who profess to love Him regard Him too often as a furious Father, who seeks only to punish and to revenge Himself for the evil that is done "against Him"—One who cannot abide the slightest contradiction but will immediately mark it down for retribution, and will not let a farthing of the debt go unpaid.

This is not the God, the Father of our Lord Jesus Christ, who Himself "hides" our sins (*dissimulans peccata*) and gets them out of sight, like a mother making quick and efficient repairs on the soiled face of a child just before entering a house where he ought to appear clean. The blessings of the ashes know Him only as the "God who desires not the death of the sinner," "who is moved by humiliation and appeased by satisfaction." He is everywhere shown to us as "plenteous in mercy—*multum misericors.*"

And from the infinite treasure of His mercies He draws forth the gift of compunction. This is a sorrow without servile fear, which is all the more deep and tender as it receives pardon from the tranquil, calm love of the merciful Lord: a love which the Latin liturgy calls, in two untranslatable words, *serenissima pietas*. The God of Ash Wednesday is like a calm sea of mercy. In Him there is no anger.

This "hiding" of God's severity is not a subterfuge. It is a revelation of His true nature. He is not severe, and it is not theologically accurate to say that He becomes angry, that He is moved to hurt and to punish.

He is love. Love becomes severe only to those who make Him severe for themselves. Love is hard only to those who refuse Him. It is not, and cannot be, Love's will to be refused. Therefore it is not and cannot be Love's will to be severe and to punish.

But it is of the very nature of Love that His absence is sorrow and death and punishment. His severity flows not from His own nature but from the fact of our refusal. Those who refuse Him are severe to themselves, and immolate themselves to the blood-thirsty god of their own self-love.

It is from this idol that Love would deliver us. To such bitter servitude, Love would never condemn us.

This brings us to the meaning of the Lenten fast. It is not that food is evil, or that natural satisfactions are something God grudgingly allows us, preferring to deprive us of them when He can.

Fasting is a good thing because food itself is a good thing. But the good things of this world have this about them, that they are good in their season and not out of it. Food is good, but to be constantly eating is a bad thing and in fact it is not even pleasant. The man who gorges himself with food and drink enjoys his surfeiting much less than the fasting person enjoys his frugal collation.

Even the fast itself, in moderation and according to God's will, is a pleasant thing. There are healthy natural joys in self-restraint: joys of the spirit which shares its lightness even with the flesh. Happy is the man whose flesh does not burden his spirit but rests only lightly upon its arm, like a graceful companion.

That is why there is wisdom in fasting. The clear head and the light step of the one who is not overfed enable him to see his way and to travel through life with a wiser joy. There is even a profound natural rightness in this fast at the spring of the year.

These reasons are true as far as they go, but they are not in themselves a sufficient explanation of the Lenten fast. Fasting is not merely a natural and ethical discipline for the Christian. It is true that St Paul

evokes the classic comparison of the athlete in train-
ing, but the purpose of the Christian fast is not
simply to tone up the system, to take off useless
fat, and get the body as well as the soul in trim
for Easter. The religious meaning of the Lenten
fast is deeper than that. Our fasting is to be seen
in the context of life and death, and St Paul made
clear that he brought his body into subjection not
merely for the good of the soul, but that the whole
man might not be "cast away." In other words the
Christian fast is something essentially different from
a philosophical and ethical discipline for the good
of the mind. It has a part in the work of salvation, and therefore in the Paschal mystery. The
Christian must deny himself, whether by fasting or in
some other way, in order to make clear his participation, and therefore in the Paschal mystery. The
the mystery of our burial with Christ in order to rise
with Him to a new life. This cannot be merely a
matter of "interior acts" and "good intentions." It is
not supposed to be something purely "mental" and
subjective. That is why fasting is proposed to the
Christian by long tradition and by the Bible itself
as a concrete way of expressing one's self-denial in
imitation of Christ and in participation with His
mysteries.

It is true that the present discipline of the Church,
for serious reasons, has alleviated the obligation of
fasting and in some areas has done away with it altogether. But certainly the Christian should desire, if
he is able, to participate in this ancient Lenten ob-

servance which is so necessary for a genuine under-standing of the meaning of the Paschal Mystery.

Finally, the ashes themselves are spiritual medi-cine, like all the sacramentals. The fruits of these apparently sterile ashes are wonderfully rich! Great is the secret power imparted to them by the influence of the risen body of Christ, who by His victory has become "life-giving Spirit."

The riches of this sacramental are clear from the prayers of the blessing. Blessed and sanctified by the sign of the cross, the ashes become a *"remedium salubre"* (health-giving medicine) and they bring *sanitas* (wholeness, cleanness) to the body as well as protection to the soul (*animae tutelam*), both of these availing for the remission of sins. They bring the grace of that humility which they signify, they bring also the pardon which we implore by the fact of receiving them.

They bring at the same time a realization of the horror of sin, and confidence of forgiveness. They bring with them all the aids necessary for the holy war of Lent, and they impart a special efficacy to our Lenten penances and prayers.

In a word, the ashes sign our whole being with the merciful blessing of God.

Armed with the grace of this great sacramental we begin a four-day preparation for Lent. For, as some may be surprised to learn, Ash Wednesday is not the beginning of Lent, but only the beginning of the Lenten fast.

The liturgical time of Lent begins on the following Sunday, and here the liturgy has a different character.

It is more ancient and therefore more objective. The structure of the Sunday Mass is loftier and more noble in its splendidly simple architecture. Nothing is said about how a sinner feels, and the question of any possible conflict between the mercy and justice of God is not raised. All is bathed in the same pure light, the light of the wilderness where Christ the Lord fasts in solitude and is tempted by the devil.

The dramatic, medieval rites of Ash Wednesday may perhaps make a stronger and more immediate appeal to our feelings. The Mass of the first Sunday however leads us deeper into the real mystery of Lent, uniting us more profoundly and more directly with the Christ who, praying and fasting in us, will purify us and offer us together with Himself to the Father in the glory of His Easter victory.

[1958]

8

CHRISTIAN SELF-DENIAL

Jesus Christ, Who commanded His disciples to leave all things, take up their cross and follow Him, insisted that He was not of this world (John 8:23). The reason is clear. The "world," in this New Testament sense, refers to the society of those who would not and could not know the Living God. That is to say that although they might have conceptual knowledge *about* God and might indeed place Him at the center of their cosmic outlook and pay Him the respect of their worship, their life was such that it could in fact dispense with the "living and efficacious" intervention of His word. In fact their religion, their philosophy —or else their absence of either—was not a confession of dependence on God, still less a way of obedience to His commands, but a way of existence that justified itself by its implicit belief in man without God. This way of existence is the "way of the flesh," that is to say the way of obedience to the "will of the flesh" or man's will to self-assertion apart from God. An asceticism that fits into this context of "flesh" may indeed by very rigorous, extremely "spiritual." What marks it as "flesh" is its sustained appetite for a definitively self-achieved "perfection," independently of our condition of creaturehood. "For all that is in the world is concupiscence of the flesh and the concupiscence of the eyes and the pride of life which is not of the Father but is of this world" (I John 2:16). Jesus told His disciples that even the professionally pious, the Pharisees, whose lives were rigid and externally austere, had made themselves incapable of receiving His word and His Holy Spirit because they "judged according to the flesh" (John 8:15), and He added: "it is the Spirit that quickeneth. The flesh profiteth nothing." (John 6:64.)

Now this Spirit of God is called by Jesus "the Spirit of Truth, which the world cannot receive because it seeth him not nor knoweth him" (John 14:27). It is the Spirit of Truth that is opposed to the "will of the flesh." And here we must try to distinguish the Biblical concept of man from the Platonic view which has become almost inseparable from it in Western thought. The Bible does not divide man into a spiritual essence (soul) and an accidental body made of existence and neither of course does Orthodox Christian theology. Yet in the tradition of Christian Platonism, magnificent though it may be, Biblical anthropology has tended to take on a Greek coloring. The true life of man is said to be the life of the soul as *distinct from and opposed to* the life of the body. Christian asceticism comes to be seen as the liberation of the soul from a kind of "imprisonment" in the body. Temporal things, belonging to the realm of the body, are either evil or at best inferior to the spiritual things in the realm of the soul and of eternity. The "spiritual life" of man is then a withdrawal from time into eternity, and this in turn implies neglect of or contempt for the ordinary temporal active life of everyday. "Spirituality" then seems to demand the negation of everyday reality and a withdrawal into a realm of angels and pure essences, where eventually "union with God" will be attained outside time and beyond the contamination of all that is bodily and temporal.

Is this a genuinely Christian perspective? Is the function of self-denial merely to "liberate the soul" and withdraw it from temporal distractions and cares? Is not Christianity rather a humble and realistic acceptance of everyday life and of God's will in a spirit of obedience and liberty? Is not the true function of our self-denial the *clarification* of God's will in our regard, and the *unification* of our whole being, body and soul, in His service?

Those who are quickened to a divine life in Christ, by His Spirit, enter into intimate communion with the Truth. They possess the Truth. Truth lives in their entire being and manifests itself in all their activities, body and soul. The "Truth has made them free." Christ Himself is the Truth. And to achieve this union with Him, this freedom based on true values and firm adhesion to God's will, we must necessarily purge out of our hearts all attachment to false ego-centered values and all reliance on our own will. For there is no freedom in selfishness, only captivity. And there is no saving vision in the unaided intellect of fallen man. The limited truths he can still perceive seem to serve only to blind him, since in practice he never turns them to the one thing that matters, the glory of God.

Every page of the New Testament forces us to accept the conclusion which St Paul expressed in such unequivocal language: "We are debtors not to the flesh (i.e., the ego-centered self), to live according to the flesh, for if you live according to the flesh you shall die, but if by the Spirit you mortify the deeds of the flesh, you shall live" (Romans 8:12–13).

There are still too many people who think that Christian abnegation means giving up all the best things in life in order to pay off a grudging debt to a severe Judge in Heaven, Who has a claim on us because we have sinned, and Who means to exact punishment by depriving us of a happiness to which we would otherwise be fully entitled. Even those who believe in a God of love are capable of making the same mistake, in a subtler and more roundabout way. God, they know, is a God of love. He wants us to be happy. But (and here is where the mistake comes in) they argue that therefore He cannot really want us to deny ourselves after all. You see, they, too, think that our happiness consists in the affirmation of the "flesh" in ego-centered satisfactions. They too, perhaps unconsciously, tend to base many of their practical decisions on what St Paul calls the "wisdom of the flesh."

From the few lines of Scripture we have quoted, and from the text in which they are embedded, it is easy to see that far from making us unhappy, Christian self-denial is supposed to help us find perfect happiness by leading us rapidly to the fulfillment of our supernatural destiny. The principles on which St John of the Cross bases his doctrine in the *Ascent of Mount Carmel* are doubtless rather strong meat. Nevertheless, those principles remain both clear and true. When the Spanish Carmelite says: "In order to arrive at having pleasure in everything, desire to have pleasure in nothing," he is teaching us the quickest way to happiness. The second half of his sentence is so bluntly stated that it may perhaps shock us into forgetting the first. But it is nevertheless true that the passions and desires of fallen human nature, because of their tendency to blind and weaken and exhaust the soul, constantly prevent us from fulfilling our highest capacities and therefore frustrate the need for happiness which is implanted in us all. It has been the constant and uninterrupted teaching of the Fathers and Doctors of the Church since the very first days of Christianity that a life without asceticism is a life of illusion, unreality, and unhappiness.

However, though it may be quite true that the genuine happiness of the human person is only attained when the self breaks out of its own narrow limits and is delivered from fixation upon its own satisfaction and affirmation, this is not the reason for Christian self-denial. There can be a genuine Christian *Eudaimonism,* or philosophy of happiness, and there is certainly such a thing as Christian humanism. An apologetic appeal to these values may be legitimate and may perhaps help to defend the Church against the accusation of remaining bogged down in Medievalism (as if there had been no happiness in the Middle Ages!). However, even if self-denial did not bring with it a certain satisfaction and an enlargement of our human capacities, it would still be necessary, because without it the Christian life cannot be fully centered on the essential obedience we owe to God, not only as our Creator but also as our Redeemer.

The call to "do penance" is based not on the fact that penance will keep us in trim, but on the fact that "the Kingdom of Heaven is at hand." Our penance— *metanoia*—is our response to the proclamation of the Gospel message, the *Kerygma* which announces our salvation if we will hear God and not harden our hearts. The function of penance and self-denial is then *contrition,* or the "breaking up" of that hardness of heart which prevents us from understanding God's command to love, and from obeying it effectively.

In order to do this we have to check and control all those impulses of that other "law in our members" which, as a matter of unpleasant practical fact, conflicts with the law of love and of grace. "The wisdom of the flesh is an enemy to God: for it is not subject to the law of God, neither can it be." (Romans 8:7).

However, no one can really embrace the Christian asceticism mapped out in the New Testament, unless he has some idea of the positive, constructive function of self-denial. The Holy Spirit never asks us to renounce anything without offering us something much higher and much more perfect in return. Self-chastisement for its own sake has no place in Christianity. The function of self-denial is to lead us to a positive increase of spiritual energy and life. The Christian dies, not merely in order to die but in order to live. And when he takes up his cross to follow Christ, the Christian realizes, or at least believes, that he is not going to die to anything but death. The Cross is the sign of Christ's victory over death. The Cross is the sign of life. It is the trellis upon which grows the Mystical Vine whose life is infinite joy and whose branches we are. If we want to share the life of that Vine we must grow on the same trellis and must suffer the same pruning. Even healthy shoots of natural life and energy, fruitful branches of our humanity, will have to be cut away. It is not only the evil that is in us that must be renounced. We are even asked to give up many good things: but only in order to get something better. "I am the true vine and my Father is the husbandman . . . every branch that beareth fruit, he will purge it, *that it may bring forth more fruit.*" (John 15:1–2). It would scarcely be reasonable to suppose that the vintner attacks the vine with his clippers because he has a grudge against it, and wants to deprive it of its due.

There is no better or more complete source of ascetical theology than the Liturgy. Quite apart from the teaching in the Psalms and Bible texts, which are the actual word of God, the Church offers us in her collects and other prayers a most exhaustive and monumental theology of self-denial and supernatural living. To *live* the Mass that we all offer by active and intelligent participation is the normal expression of Christian metanoia.

Christian asceticism is remarkable above all for its balance, its sense of proportion. It does not overstress the negative side of the ascetic life, nor does it tend to flatter the ego by diminishing responsibilities or watering down the truth. It shows us clearly that while we can do nothing without grace, we must nevertheless co-operate with grace. It warns us that we must make an uncompromising break with the world and all that it stands for, but it keeps encouraging us to understand that our existence in "the world" and in time becomes fruitful and meaningful in proportion as we are able to assume spiritual and Christian responsiblity for our life, our work, and even for the world we live in. Thus Christian asceticism does not provide a flight from the world, a refuge from the stress and distraction of manifold wickedness. It enables us to enter into the confusion of the world bearing something of the light of Truth in our hearts, and capable of exercising something of the mysterious, transforming power of the Cross, of love and of sacrifice.

But in that case, self-denial must mean something more than the triumph of our good self over our evil self, of reason over compulsion, or even more naively, of "soul" over "body." Actually it is not a question of resolving a conflict between two forces in ourselves but of submitting our whole being to the will of God in the "obedience of faith." This means much more than simply doing good and avoiding evil, much more than simply acquiring inner peace, and certainly more than just becoming thoroughly respectable and pious. It means entering into the Paschal Mystery of the death and resurrection of Christ by the total conversion of our entire self to Him by the Cross and a new life.

Liturgy is a ritual participation in the death of Christ (by which all our sins are expiated) and in His glorious Resurrection (by which His divine life is made our own) and in His Ascension (by which we enter with Him into heaven and sit at the right hand of the Father). We who offer the Holy Sacrifice and who receive into our hearts the Body and Blood of the Savior are building the Kingdom of Heaven on earth and in history. It is still a heaven possessed only in the darkness of faith and hope: yet the love by which Jesus unites us to Himself gives us a profound, sweet and experiential certitude of the union of our lives with His life and with one another in Him. We are already citizens of that Jerusalem that needs no sun and no moon because Christ is the lamp thereof. Here, for instance, is what a postcommunion, chosen at random in the Missal, tells us about the divine life we are already leading on earth. The Church addresses the Blessed Trinity in these words, after the people of God have received the Body and Blood of the Risen Savior: "Lord, may the action of this heavenly gift possess our minds and bodies so that our natural way of doing things may no longer prevail in us, but that the effects of this Communion may always dominate our lives." (15th Sunday after Pentecost.)

Here we can see, first of all, that the Church clearly recognizes what her task is. God has placed in her hands divine instruments for our conversion and sanctification—the Sacraments. In fact, it is He Himself who, through the Church, works in our lives by means of these Sacraments. What is He doing in our lives? He is gradually taking over everything that we have and everything that we are, in order to gain complete possession of our souls, bodies and all our faculties, elevating them above the natural level and transforming them in His will. In other words, He is substituting His life for our life, His thoughts for our thoughts, His will for our will. This process of transformation leads to the end for which we were created —perfect union with God. It is only when we are perfectly united to Him that we become our true selves. It is only in Him that we can finally appreciate the true value of His creation. If he seems to deprive us of natural goods, we will find them all restored to us a hundredfold in Him.

Often in the course of the liturgical year the Church complains, in our behalf, that we are pressed down under the burden of our own human activity. That seems strange! To be free to do things in our own way would appear, at first sight, to be "the liberty of the sons of God." But no. As we enter into the ascetic life and advance in the ways of self-denial, we find that our biggest obstacle and our biggest burden is this old man of the sea, this body of death, this inescapable *self* we carry around with us. He is not our real self at all. He is the caricature of what we ought to be. But he rides us without mercy and, without the all-powerful help of God, we will never be able to shake him off. And he is the one who makes us act according to the "wisdom of the flesh." He is the father of all our worldiness. He is the one who prevents our liberation from "the world," and our transformation in Christ. He is the one who makes our life and work in the world a sterile and trivial assertion of our own futility.

And so we must remember that our asceticism is not directed against created things as such. Our real enemy is within our own castle. It is only because this enemy surrounds himself with the images and sensations and delights of created things and thus fortifies himself against all efforts of grace to dislodge him, that we must necessarily control our natural love for good things in order to fight him. When the Church prays, as she does, that God may give us the grace to despise earthly things and desire the things of heaven, she does not mean to imply that creation is evil: but that an ego-centered love of the good things of life is a source of darkness and evil in the world.

How does the liturgy look at created things? Everybody knows that the Church, realizing that all creation fell with Adam, intends to raise up all creation together with man, in the New Adam, Christ. It was in Christ that all things were made in the first place. "For in him were all things created in heaven and on earth . . . and he is before all and by him all things consist" (Col. 1:16–17). To deliver creation from the power of evil, the Church has only to associate created things in man's worship of the Creator. Thus they begin once more to serve the purpose for which they were created—to lift man up, body and soul, to God. "For every creature of God is good, and nothing is to be rejected that is received with thanksgiving: *for it is sanctified by the word of God and prayer.*" (I Tim.

4:4) Just take a glance at the liturgy of the Paschal Vigil at the *Exsultet* (where the bees come in for their measure of praise) and at the blessing of the font (where the Church becomes positively enthusiastic about water, calling it a "holy and innocent creature"). All this tells us what respect the Church has for God's creation. But the fact remains that she has no respect whatever either for the "world" or for the "flesh" and least of all for the devil. These three forces produce mental attitudes, ways of looking at things and doing things, which must be rooted clean out of the Christian life. Self-denial is then directed to this process of uprooting and liberation.

There are two extremes to be avoided. On one hand there is the error of those who believe that creation is evil and who therefore seek salvation and sanctity in an exaggerated asceticism that tries to sever the soul entirely from the rest of creation. This is the spiritual disease called "angelism." But on the other hand there is the error of those who act as if divine charity made no practical demands on human conduct: as if grace were merely a quality injected into our natural lives, making them automatically pleasing and meritorious in the sight of God, without any obligation on our part to live on the supernatural level of faith and Christian virtue. This attitude sometimes usurps the name of "humanism." Concerning those who cherish this view, the twelfth century Cistercian, St Aelred of Rievaulx, wrote sardonically: "Although they do not say 'Let us eat, drink and be merry, for tomorrow we die!' they say

'Let us eat, drink and be merry for we are full of charity!' "

True sanctity does not consist in trying to live without creatures. It consists in using the goods of life in order to do the will of God. It consists in using God's creation in such a way that everything we touch and see and use and love gives new glory to God. To be a saint means to pass through the world gathering fruits for heaven from every tree and reaping God's glory in every field. The saint is one who is in contact with God in every possible way, in every possible direction. He is united to God in the depths of his own being. He sees and touches God in everything and everyone around him. Everywhere he goes, the world rings and resounds (though silently) with the deep pure harmonies of God's glory.

But God cannot be glorified by anything that violates the order established by His wisdom. This order demands that man's body, and all that his body uses, be in subjection to his soul, and that man's soul be subject to God. Now this order is absolutely impossible, in our present state, without the generous and even severe practice of mortification. This order has been turned completely upside down by sin. The man who is outside the orbit of God's grace is not normally governed by reason but by passion. The mere possession of grace does not entirely deliver us from this state. It only puts in our hands the weapons by which we must win our freedom, helped by the power of God, through the merits of Christ's Cross, in His Holy Spirit. But the power of Calvary cannot avail in a life that does not in some measure enter into the mystery of Christ's Passion and death and Resurrection. "If any man will come after me, let him deny himself and take up his cross and follow me." (Matt. 16:24). "They that are Christ's have crucified their flesh with its vices and concupiscences." (Galatians 5:24).

We cannot use created things for the glory of God unless we are in control of ourselves. We cannot be in control of ourselves if we are under the power of the desires and appetites and passions of the flesh. We cannot give ourselves to God if we do not belong to ourselves. And we do not belong to ourselves if we belong to our own ego.

The real purpose of Christian asceticism is then not to liberate the soul from the desires and needs of the body, but to bring the whole man into complete submission to God's will as expressed in the concrete demands of life in all its existential reality. A spirituality that merely entrenched a man in the privacy of his own will and his own ego beyond the reach of all the claims of flesh, of history and of time, would not only be futile, but it might also confirm him in the evil of that spurious autonomy which is deaf to the call to salvation and obedience uttered in the Gospel Kerygma.

Self-denial is useless unless it opens the ears of our heart to obey the will of God commanding us to take our place in time, in history and in the work of building His Kingdom of Love and Truth. An asceticism that fails in this may actually strengthen our opposition and resistance to God by making us concentrate on our own autonomy and moral perfection instead of on the concrete obligation to love God and our fellow man.

St Gregory Nazianzen speaks of the Christian as an "instrument played by the Holy Spirit." The aim of asceticism is to keep this instrument in tune. Mortification is not simply the progressive control of instinct by deadening the appetites of the heart. That is too crude a view. It is rather like the tightening of a violin string. We do not just go on twisting and twisting until the string breaks. That would not be sanctity, but insanity. No: what we must do is bring the strings of the delicate instrument, which is our whole being to the exact pitch which the Holy Spirit desires of us, in order that He may produce in us the exquisite melody of divine love that we were created to sing before the face of our heavenly Father.

False asceticism is not in tune with the Holy Ghost because it is a perversion of grace. And it is also a perversion of nature. It frustrates God's work and diminishes all our natural and supernatural capacities for good. The false ascetic is usually one who develops a kind of split personality. One half of his personality takes up arms against the other half and tries to destroy it. But this does not succeed. What happens then? The suppressed half of this unfortunate being withdraws into the "depths of the soul," and there healthy natural tendencies turn into unhealthy and vicious dispositions. That is why those who go about their self-denial in a crude and inhuman way are often proud, irritable and gross. That is why men who might have been saints have become fanatics, have persecuted the saints, and burned them at the stake.

Self-denial can assuredly bring peace to the soul that is troubled by all the cares, worries, sorrows and unrest that follow inevitably from attachment to created things. Asceticism roots out every plant from which the fruits of anxiety grow. The ascetic, then, should be a tranquil and happy man. His will be a simple and limpid soul, like a pool of clear water into which the sunlight of God's presence can enter without obstacle, to illumine and penetrate all. But this tranquility depends on the virtue of discretion. God demands that all Christians deny themselves but He does not ask the same kind of renunciation from a housewife with ten children as from a Cistercian monk—or vice versa! In the long run, it might well happen that the housewife might turn out to be more mortified than the monk: but she is not expected to do penance in exactly the same way. Her self-denial will be measured by the duties of her state as a wife and as a mother.

However, we must not imagine that the way of self-denial is always a way of tranquility and uninterrupted peace. It does not resolve all doubts and deliver us from every care as if by magic. Self-denial attunes us to the Spirit of God and the Spirit may not always sing a tune that harmonizes with our nature. There may be terrible discords instead of tranquil harmonies. Self-denial brings order into our lives sometimes in the form of an apparent disorder, and we may sometimes have to find peace as best we can in the midst of confusion. What matters is not the

tranquility of our own heart but the sincerity of our
faith and the totality of our obedience to God. But
before we can begin to obey Him we must first recognize how profoundly inclined we are to disobey, and
how difficult it really is for us to embrace a way of
obedience to grace that means letting go of the security of our own self-hood and our own nature.

That is why the desire for ascetic works that pacify
our minds and give us a sense of achievement may in
fact prove to be an escape from the true and radical
self-denial required of us by God.

Whatever may be the mode and measure of self-
denial that God asks of us (and this is a matter that
cannot really be decided without prayer and spiritual
direction), all Christian asceticism is characterized by
wholeness and by balance. Christ admits of no division. He who is not with Jesus is against Him. There
is no fellowship between light and darkness, between
the temple of God and idols. God asks us to give Him
everything. But we have already said what that
means: using all creatures for God alone. Consequently our asceticism must always be balanced. The
true ascetic is not one who never relaxes, but one who
relaxes at the right time and in the right measure,
who orders his whole life, under the direct guidance
of the Holy Spirit, so that he works when God wants
him to work, rests when God wants him to rest and
prays constantly through it all by a simple and loving
gaze that keeps his heart and mind united with the
indwelling Spirit.

To such a one the Cross is always a source of
strength and peace. "Because I am nailed to the Cross

with Christ," says St Thomas Aquinas, paraphrasing St Paul and commenting on him, "because I am nailed to the Cross with Christ I have power to do good." Without the Cross, there is little spiritual vitality in our labors for God and His Church.

In a world in which there is so much involuntary suffering, it is not strange that there should be many men and women who begin to discover in themselves a totally unfamiliar desire to take upon themselves penances and mortifications for which there is no strict obligation. Wherever the Spirit of God works, He draws men away from the "wisdom of the flesh." Pleasures and achievements that once delighted their spirit now turn to ashes as soon as they are savored, and it becomes a pleasure for these Christians to do without the good things that most men have come to consider almost indispensable.

At the same time they become deeply aware of the radical insufficiency of arbitrarily chosen "ascetic practices" and of "methods" which are simply aimed at resolving moral conflicts within the self and establishing the ego in a peaceful equilibrium. The true self-denial of the Christian is not a conquest of himself by himself, but a dying to self in order to live to God in Christ. This is the great question that preoccupied St. Paul—the problem of seeking salvation by the works of the law instead of by grace. Our salvation is not to be found in asceticism alone but in the Cross of Christ. Self-denial, however rigorous, lacks all Christian meaning apart from the Cross and Resurrection of Christ.

This is why Lent is a season of mortification and

renouncement: not just because Christians discovered that a little fasting in Springtime was good for their constitutions, but because their fasts, renunciations and alms deeds had an essential part to play as signs of a full participation in the Easter Mystery.

The Church has relaxed the general laws of fasting in Lent, but this does not mean that Lent has now ceased to be a season of fasting and self-denial. It remains for the individual Christian, in the sincerity of his own conscience before God, to undertake such acts of self-denial and charity as will truly signify his will to die to himself and live in the Spirit of the Risen Christ.

[1950]

9

COMMUNITY OF PARDON

God reveals Himself to the world in the Mystical Christ, the Church, which is the community of those who are reconciled to the Father, in Christ, because they are united with one another in the Holy Spirit. If the unity of Christians in One Body makes the Church a sign of God in the world, and if men tend unfortunately to conflict and division by reason of their weakness, selfishness and sin, then the will to reconciliation and pardon is necessary if the Church is to make God visible in the world. Nor can this pardon, this communion in forgiveness, remain interior and invisible. It must be clearly manifest. So the mystery of the Church demands that Christians love one another in a visible and concrete way—and that they love all men.

Christ will not be visible to the world in His Church except in proportion as Christians seek peace and unity with one another and with all men. But since conflict is inevitable, unity cannot be maintained except in great difficulty, with constantly renewed sacrifice, with lucid honesty, openness, humility, the readiness to ask forgiveness and to forgive. Christian life is a perpetual conversion, a turning to God and to the Church of pardon.

In so far as the Church is a community of pardon it is an epiphany of the Divine Love, Agape: the Love that underlies the mystery of creation and of redemption. This love is the key to everything, but it cannot be known, discovered or understood by rational investigation alone. It must be revealed to men in a free gift of God. It is revealed to them in the gift of love. God has willed that men should know Him not in esoteric secrets and strange philosophies, but in the announcement of the Gospel message which is the message of His love. "This is my commandment, that you love one another as I have loved you" (John 15:12) "You have not chosen me but I have chosen you, and have appointed you that you should go and bear fruit . . . These things I command you that you may love one another." (id. 16–17) The love of Christians, commanded by God and carried out by them, makes them "God's workmanship." (Ephesians 2:10)

This is more than a message, for if it remains only a matter of words it cannot be fully received and fully understood. The word of the Gospel is understood only when it is obeyed. It is known to those who strive to practice it. Yet it is also more than a moral doctrine that can be preached by example. To receive the word of the Gospel, the Kerygma of God's love for man in Christ, of God's gift of Himself to man in Christ, is to enter into the living and active communion of love which has become the center of salvation history. This communion itself is a profound religious mystery, for it is participation not only in a natural love of man for his brother, but in the love of God for sinful man as revealed in the mystery of the Cross and Resurrection of Jesus Christ.

To enter fully into this mystery one must receive the Holy Spirit, who is the Love of God (I Cor. 2:10–12). The Holy Spirit dwells in the Church, giving life to all who live in Christ, as members of His Church. The Holy Spirit gives light and love to those who are enlightened by the word of the Gospel and who seek truth and life in Jesus Christ. The Holy Spirit, Who is the bond of union between the Father and the Son, is also the bond of union between the faithful who have been reconciled to the Father through the Son, and with one another in the Church.

Before His death on the Cross, Jesus told His disciples that He would soon come to them not visibly but in the Holy Spirit, and would dwell in them by His Spirit. "I will not leave you orphans, I will come to you. Yet a little while and the world no longer sees me. But you see me, for I live and you shall live. In that day you shall know that I am in the Father, and you in me and I in you." (John 14:18–20) "When the Advocate (the Paraclete, the Holy Spirit) has come, whom I will send you from the Father, the Spirit of Truth who proceeds from the Father, he will bear witness concerning me." (John 15:26–27)

As Christ passed through death to life in the Spirit (I Peter 3:18) so the Christian follows Christ on His Paschal Mystery through death to life. Sin is pardoned, man is redeemed not by the destruction and punishment of man's freedom, but by its purification. It is precisely in his *freedom* that man accepts the redemptive power of the Cross. It is man's freedom that is nailed to the Cross with Christ and rises to new life in the Christian agape. That is to say that each individual renounces what is purely selfish and confesses his wrong, in order to find himself on the new spiritual level of reconciliation in Christ. But no one sincerely confesses his own sin without at the same time pardoning his brother. (Matthew 18:23–35) Forgiveness of sins is proclaimed to the world in Christ, and is granted to each one who, in the act of seeking pardon, himself pardons others and makes himself an instrument of the divine mercy. Sin cannot be pardoned and healed without love, because all sin is, at its root, a refusal of love. No matter how great our sin may be, it is forgiven when we consent to love. (Luke 7:47) The Sacrament of penance is instituted as the visible sign of this reconciliation and hence it is required that we receive it before we return from mortal sin to Eucharistic Communion, the sign of our life in Christ's love.

The Gospel is then a message of reconciliation in the Spirit of Love. Those who receive the Holy Spirit are reconciled to God and to one another in love. The supreme purpose of all life is then to receive the Holy Spirit, to live by the Spirit of Christ, to have Him dwelling and acting in our hearts. (John 7:37–39) And it is for this that the Spirit awakens in our hearts faith in Christ and draws us to the Church, which is the Living Body of Christ. When we live as members of Christ, we receive the Holy Spirit. The sacraments of the Church give us participation in the life of the Spirit. Faith awakens that life in our hearts. Love is the guarantee that the life of the Spirit is growing in us. He who confesses Christ and loves his brother, who forgets himself in order to help his brother and who devotes his life to the truth of the Gospel, lives and grows in the Spirit. Love is the sign of the Holy Spirit at work in the Church and in the world.

"Everyone who loves is born of God, and knows God. He who does not love, does not know God; for God is love. In this has the love of God been shown in our case, that God has sent His only begotten Son into the world that we may live through Him. In this is the love, not that we have loved God, but that He has first loved us, and sent His Son a propitiation for our sins. Beloved, if God has so loved us, we also ought to love one another. No one has ever seen God. If we love one another, God abides in us and His love is perfected in us. In this we know that we abide in Him and He in us, *because He has given us of His Spirit.*" (I John 4:7–13)

But we are not yet perfect in love. As long as we are on earth we remain sinful and imperfect men. Even though the Holy Spirit dwells in the hearts of all who have faith in Christ and seek to keep His commandment of love, yet at the same time there is in these hearts the capacity and indeed the tendency to sin. Not only that, but those who love God sincerely can still, through weakness, error, confusion, and infidelity, fall into sin. This is in fact the great problem and scandal of Christian frailty. Yet it should not be a scandal. It becomes a scandal when the true nature of the Church as a community of pardon and reconciliation is obscured, and when it is replaced by the idea of a Church that saves sinners without herself being composed of men capable of sin, indeed of sinners.

There are certainly the Gospel parables which show us the Church made up of wheat and cockle, wise and foolish virgins. But this is not the same as saying that the Church is divided into two easily recognizable *classes* of saints and sinners—as if one were more or less predestined to live a life clearly defined as being one or the other. Certainly there are men and women in the Church, both religious and laypeople, who live holy lives and avoid all serious sin. It is obligatory for all Christians to seek to live without sin. And yet the fact remains that however virtuous we may be, our virtues do not deliver us from the condition of "sinners" who often fail, make mistakes, give in to frailty, or allow ourselves to be deceived by appearances of good. No man is infallible and impeccable. We all need the mercy of God, we all need the pardon and love of our neighbor.

Furthermore all *realize*, or should realize, this frailty and fallibility in themselves. All should *feel* in the depths of their heart the accusing presence of nothingness and death which gives the lie to their vain image of themselves, their foolish and unsubstantial projects for a happiness centered in themselves. In fact, the lives of those who have been truly close to God have taught us that the saints are the ones who more than all others felt in themselves the evil of sin and the need for pardon.

The Church militant then is entirely made up of men who recognize themselves to be sinners in need of reconciliation and pardon, and not of two impossible classes: those who have become impeccable and can judge others, and those who are trying (or should try) to become impeccable so that they will not be judged any more by the perfect.

But where shall the sinner turn for pardon? To God, obviously. And the first thing is of course to seek Him in the depths of our heart, asking pardon for our sins. But the Christian conscience, enlightened by the Holy Spirit, tells us that this inner movement of repentance in the privacy of the heart, though it is essential, is not enough by itself. For sin is not a purely individual affair, and neither is pardon. However private it may be, sin remains in some sense everybody's business because everyone is affected by the evil that is in the heart of one. It is not possible for man to live so separated from others, so isolated and private in his own heart, that his secret selfishness and sin will not affect others. We are involved in each other's lives, not by choice but by necessity, for that is the way we are made. No man can pretend successfully to live purely in his own private universe and remain sane. The very condition of normal human life is community, communication, and "conversation" in the old Latin sense of *conversatio*, exchange on the level of social living. The lives of all men are inextricably mixed together, and the salvation and damnation of souls is involved in this inescapable

communication of freedoms. Either we will love and
help one another or we will hate and attack one
another, in which latter case we will all be one
another's hell. Perhaps Sartre was not far wrong in
saying that where freedom is abused, society itself
turns into hell. (*"L'enfer c'est les autres."*)

The heart of the Christian message is precisely
reconciliation in the Spirit of Love so that communion in freedom turns to communion in beati-
tude. In which case heaven is communion with
"others."

Therefore the Church possesses a great gift of God
in the Sacrament of Penance. The sinner confesses his
sin to another man who, however, listens to his confession not as man but as a representative of Christ,
indeed as Christ. Because our sins concern the whole
Body of Christ they must be confessed to another and
forgiven by another in order for our reconciliation to
Christ in His Church to be complete. And in this
Sacrament the Holy Spirit is given to the forgiven
one. He is restored to life in Christ. His spirit is
healed by the presence of the Divine Paraclete. He
can return to the altar of God and renew his spiritual
joy in the Eucharistic banquet.

2.

We must in all things seek God. But we do not seek
Him the way we seek a lost object, a "thing." He is
present to us in our heart, our personal subjectivity,
and to seek Him is to recognize this fact. Yet we
cannot be aware of it as a reality unless He reveals

His presence to us. He does not reveal Himself simply in our own heart. He reveals Himself to us through one another. He reveals Himself to us in the Church, in the community of believers, in the *koinonia* of those who trust Him and love Him.

Seeking God is not just an operation of the intellect, or even a contemplative illumination of the mind. We seek God by striving to surrender ourselves to Him whom we do not see, but Who is in all things and through all things and above all things.

We seek God by surrendering ourselves to His will. But His will is not just a matter of blind decrees and laws external to ourselves. It is the law of love which is implanted in every nature, and the revelation of spiritual love in personal freedom. The fruit of this love is the restoration of all things in Christ, the union of all beings with God, through man, by the exercise of man's freedom.

Man's freedom is therefore the instrument of divine redemption and reconciliation. This work of reconciliation requires the formation of a living body of men who are united by the Spirit of God. God's work is to form a living mystical body, which will be His Son, the One Christ, Head and Members, in which all the members share One Spirit, one Sonship, and are "One Christ."

For this, each member must undergo a transformation by the Holy Spirit. He must undergo a renewal in the depths of his being:

Now this I affirm and testify in the Lord, that you must no longer live as the Gentiles do, in the futility of their minds; they are darkened in their understanding, alienated from the life of God because of the ignorance that is in them, due to their hardness of heart; they have become callous 'and have given themselves up to licentiousness, greedy to practice every kind of uncleanness. You did not so learn Christ!—assuming that you have heard about him and were taught in him, as the truth is in Jesus. Put off your old nature which belongs to your former manner of life and is corrupt through deceitful lusts, and be renewed in the spirit of your minds, and put on the new nature, created after the likeness of God in true righteousness and holiness.

(Ephesians 4:17–25)

This renewal is to be seen from many points of view: as renunciation, as pardon, as conversion, as "justification," as self-surrender, as thanksgiving, "eucharistia." The word "love" in the sense of Agape perfectly covers and includes them all.

But let us remember especially that the Church is a community of pardon. All who have entered the common life of the body of Christ have done so by the way of pardon. And they remain in the Body of Christ only through pardon, through the mercy of Christ: not only of Christ, as Head, but also of Christ in His members.

The mercy and pardon of Christ must be continually at work in all the members and through all the members of the Mystical Body. This is what makes the Church truly a Mother: she gives life by gentleness, understanding, love and pardon. She forgives sins, that is to say she heals separations. Sin is separation from God, and from those who love God. Sin is a cutting off from life. It is a spiritual death, and pardon is the restoration of life. Sin is a cutting off of man's free will from communion in love and common understanding. Sin is the refusal to share, and the denial of any need to share. Pardon renews sharing, because it brings the sinner back into contact with the body which he needs, with those whose love he needs, by whose love he lives. But the sinner is also important to the Church, for the community of pardon needs the sinner and that is why she pardons him. The Church needs to share with him the good that she has received from God.

This is why the Risen Savior, on the day of His resurrection, in His first meeting with the disciples, before all else gave them the Holy Spirit and the power to grant divine pardon:

> On the evening of that day, the first day of the week, the doors being shut where the disciples were, for fear of the Jews, Jesus came and stood among them and said to them, "Peace be with you." When he had said this, he showed them his hands and his side. Then the disciples were glad when they saw the Lord. Jesus said to them again, "Peace be with you. As the Father has sent me, even so I send you." And when he had said this, he breathed on them, and said to them, "Receive the Holy Spirit. If you forgive the sins of any, they are forgiven; if you retain the sins of any, they are retained."
>
> (John 20:19–23)

This is to be seen not only as the institution of the Sacrament of Penance, which of course it is, but also as a revelation of the truth that the very life of the Body of Christ is pardon. The Spirit by which the Church lives is the Spirit of love, of unity. Unity can be preserved or restored only by understanding, acceptance and pardon. The Church is a body of men who know they are forgiven and who forgive repeatedly because they are themselves forgiven repeatedly.

The Church is then not so much a body of men who are pure and never offend, but of men who, in their weakness and frailty, frequently err and offend, but who have received from God the power to forgive one another in His name. They possess the Holy Spirit and they can give the Holy Spirit in some sense, to one another. The Holy Spirit Himself moves them to do this, and acts in them, to save others. (See Acts 8:14–18, 26–39; 10:24–48, etc.)

We, then, who form one body in Christ, share with one another the message of Christ's divine truth, we share His word, we share His worship, we share His love, we share His Spirit.

The highest adoration we offer to God, "in spirit and in truth" is in this sharing of the breath of the Divine Spirit with one another in pardon and in love. That is why we are told to forgive our brother before we go to offer sacrifice. That is why we exchange the kiss of peace before Communion. The kiss of peace is in some way a part of our Eucharistic communion: it symbolizes the spiritual sharing of the Holy Spirit. With a holy kiss we give the Holy Spirit to our brother, as if the flame of one candle were transferred to enlighten another.

The Eucharist is the celebration of our reconciliation in Christ and in His Spirit. In the Postcommunion of the Easter Mass, the Church prays God to

"Pour forth upon us the Spirit of Your love, so that You may, in Your mercy, lead those who have received the Paschal Sacraments to be of one heart." Furthermore, the Holy Spirit not only renews the hearts of all the faithful through the Eucharistic liturgy and communion, but in that Liturgy the Holy Spirit Himself is given as the remission of our sins—*quia ipse est remissio omnium peccatorum.* (Postcommunion, Tuesday of Pentecost.) In proportion as we love and pardon one another we open the whole Church to the action of the Spirit of God.

We are a community of pardon, therefore a community of penitents. But what is a penitent? Is he simply one who carries out all kinds of difficult and forbidding acts of self-punishment? This perhaps may have a place in some lives. But the true spirit of penance is inseparable from the recognition of our need for pardon, not only of God's pardon, but of our brother's pardon. We must recognize our need for the "kiss of peace" by which our brother, in his forgiveness, and his acceptance, gives us the Holy Spirit from his own heart and in which we, in our turn, share with him the love of the Holy Spirit in our own heart.

We are a community of pardon, not a community of judgment. We are told not to judge one another, and we must not. We must not judge in such a way as to reject and condemn. That is to say we must not refuse to accept the genuine good will of our brother, we must not reject his sincere and open offers of reconciliation, his true friendship. Even our enemy must not be judged, but his need for forgiveness must be recognized. We must not judge, that is to say we must always be ready to take the first step in offering reconciliation and pardon. We must not let our evaluation of a man's acts stand in the way of the Holy Spirit, who draws us to unity with the "other" in spite of his actions which make him different from ourselves, perhaps opposed to us.

We have a duty to pardon, because it is through us that God wishes to pardon all sinners.

In building a community of pardon which is the temple of God, we have to recognize that no one of us is complete, self-sufficient, perfectly holy in himself. No one can rest in his own individual virtues and interior life. No man lives for himself alone. To live for oneself alone is to die. We grow and flourish in our own lives in so far as we live for others and through others. What we ourselves lack, God has given them. They must complete us where we are deficient. Hence we must always remain open to one another so that we can always share with each other.

Often the good that is given us by God is given us only to be shared with another. If He sees that we will not pardon and will not be open, that we will not share, then the good is not given us. But to him in whom there is the greatest readiness to share with all, most is given. The greatest of gifts then is this openness, this love, this readiness to accept and to pardon and to share with others, in the Spirit of Christ. If we are open we will not only offer pardon, but will not disdain to seek it and recognize our own desperate need of it.

Openness is the sign of the Spirit's presence, for

openness is the sign of love. How characteristic was the action of Pope John XXIII who, when asked after his election what he intended to do as Pope, simply walked over to a window and flung it open.

(1963)

10

EASTER: THE NEW LIFE

Easter is not sufficiently well understood if we think of it only as the time when we reaffirm our belief that Christ rose from the dead. That the historical fact of the resurrection is the keystone of the whole structure of Christian faith is still not sufficient reason why Easter should be the great feast that it is.

Easter is not a day to be compared to the Fourth of July although it is in all truth the celebration of our Christian freedom. But this celebration does not merely recall the act by which we are liberated, it revives our freedom itself, in the renewal of the mystery in which we become free.

In any case, the Easter mystery is not celebrated only at Easter but every day in the year, because the Mass is the Paschal Mystery. Passiontide, Holy Week, Easter and the "holy fifty days" of the Easter season culminating in the celebration of Pentecost, all combine to spread the Easter mystery out before us in time in all its detail: but the fulness of Good Friday, Easter and Pentecost is also compressed within the compass of every day's Mass. For each time we participate in the sacred Mysteries, the *Pascha Domini*

(The Passover of the Lord), we die with Christ, rise with Him and receive from Him the Spirit of Promise who transforms us and unites us to the Father in and through the Son.

Lent has summoned us to change our hearts, to effect in ourselves the Christian *metanoia*. But at the same time Lent has reminded us perhaps all too clearly of our own powerlessness to change our lives in any way. Lent in the liturgical year plays the role of the Law, the pedagogue, who convinces us of sin and inflicts upon us the crushing evidence of our own nothingness. Hence it disquiets and sobers us, awakening in us perhaps some sense of that existential "dread" of the creature whose freedom suspends him over an abyss which may be an infinite meaninglessness, an unbounded despair. This is the fruit of that Law which judges our freedom together with its powerlessness to impose full meaning on our lives merely by comforming to a moral code. Is there nothing more than this?

But now the power of Easter has burst upon us with the resurrection of Christ. Now we find in ourselves a strength which is not our own, and which is freely given to us whenever we need it, raising us above the Law, giving us a new law which is hidden in Christ: the law of His merciful love for us. Now we no longer strive to be good because we have to, because it is a duty, but because our joy is to please Him who has given all His love to us! Now our life is full of meaning!

Easter is the hour of our own deliverance—from what? Precisely from Lent and from its hard Law which accuses and judges our infirmity. *We are no longer under the Law.* We are delivered from the harsh judgment!

Here is all the greatness and all the unimaginable splendor of the Easter mystery—here is the "grace" of Easter which we fail to lay hands on because we are afraid to understand its full meaning. To understand Easter and live it, we must renounce our dread of newness and of freedom!

Death exercises a twofold power in our lives: it holds us by sin, and it holds us by the Law. To die to death and live a new life in Christ we must die not only to sin *but also to the Law.*

Every Christian knows that he must die to sin. But the great truth that St Paul exhausted himself to preach in season and out is a truth that we Christians have barely grasped, a truth that has got away from us, that constantly eludes us and has continued to do so for twenty centuries. We cannot get it into our heads what it means to be no longer slaves of the Law. And the reason is that we do not have the courage to face this truth which contains in itself the crucial challenge of our Christian faith, the great reality that makes Christianity different from every other religion.

In all other religions men seek justification, salvation, escape from "the wheel of birth and death" by ritual acts, or by religious observances, or by ascetic and contemplative techniques. These are means devised by men to enable them to liberate and justify *themselves.* All the other religions impose upon man rigid and complicated laws, subject him more or less completely to prescribed exterior forms, or to what St Paul calls "elementary notions."

But Christianity is precisely a liberation from every rigid legal and religious system. This is asserted with such categorical force by St Paul, that we cease to be Christians the moment our religion becomes slavery to "the Law" rather than a free personal adherence by loving faith, to the risen and living Christ; "Do you seek justification by the Law . . . you are fallen from grace . . . In fact, in Christ Jesus neither circumcision nor its absence is of any avail. What counts is faith that expresses itself in love" (Gal. 5:4,6). And elsewhere he says that the only thing that matters for a Christian is his "new life"—the "new creature" which he has become in Christ (Gal. 6:15).

Hence the Christian has no Law but Christ. His "Law" is the new life itself which has been given to him in Christ. His Law is not written in books but in the depths of his own heart, not by the pen of man but by the finger of God. His duty is now not just to *obey* but to *live*. He does not have to save himself, he *is saved* by Christ. He must live to God in Christ, not only as one who seeks salvation but as one who *is saved*.

One might almost say that this truth is the great "scandal" of Christianity. It is the stone which is constantly being rejected by the builders. It is the element in our own faith which we fear and refuse to face, just as the Jews feared it and refused to face it in the challenge which Jesus flung at them by healing on the Sabbath, and calling Himself the "Lord of the Sabbath." Listen to St Paul:

Christ has set us free to enjoy freedom. Stand fast then and do not be caught again under the yoke of slavery . . . The Law has been our attendant . . . Since you have come to know God, or rather to be known by God, how is it that you turn back again to those weak and worthless and elementary notions and wish again to be enslaved to them?

(Gal. 5:1; 3:24; 4:9)

Translated into our terms: Easter is the mystery of our redemption. We who have died and risen with Christ *are no longer sinners*. Sin is dead in us. The Law has no further hold on us.

And yet this is not as simple as it sounds. Our new life in Christ is not a permanent and guaranteed possession, handed over to our control, a "property" which we now definitively have. We are still suspended over the abyss, and we can still fall back into the awful dread of the alienated man who has lost trust. But the fact remains that *if we consent to it,* grace and trust are renewed from moment to moment in our lives. They are not a permanent possession but an ever present gift of God's love. For this liberty to continue, we must really believe in the power of God to sanctify us and keep us saints. *We must dare to be saints by the power of God.* We must dare to have a holy respect and reverence for ourselves, as we are redeemed and sanctified by the blood of Christ. We must have the courage to grasp the great power that has been given to us, at the same time realizing that this power is always made perfect in infirmity, and that it is not a "possession."

What about our own weaknesses? What about the law in our members, the law of sin and of death?

They are still there, but we do not have to dread them. We do not have to hate ourselves because their power still works in us. This power has been rendered harmless by the victory of Christ, as long as we remain firm in our faith, and trust in His power with a deep tranquil confidence. Thus we dare to live in the apparent contradiction that we are "sinners," still not immune to dread and loss of trust, and yet marvelously sustained by the presence and grace of Christ.

This trust means a delicate and loving subjection to the guidance of His Spirit, a careful and reverent attention to every indication of His will. We must dare to "feast in the unleavened bread of sincerity and truth"—that is to say, we must be perfectly frank (in so far as one can be frank) with ourselves, with our neighbor, and with God. We no longer have to conceal anything, because our past and even our present weaknesses are no longer a cause for shame. We do not have to excuse ourselves, justify ourselves. We have no longer any need for the bitter zeal which seeks to bolster up our confidence in our own virtue by seeking out flaws in the virtue of others. Such zeal is the old leaven of *those who are under the Law.*

We have not suddenly become angels. We have been sinners and can easily become sinners again. We are still "sinners," but ones who do not sin. (I John 3:9) The fact remains that the most deadly influence in the life of the Christian is this spirit of slavery to the Law which frustrates the grace and liberty of

Christ in our souls and disposes good and holy souls
to fall back into sin. For that is precisely the function
of the Law. "The Law intervened that the offense
might become greater," said St Paul (Rom. 5:20).
The Law without Christ is a source of despair,
whereas the cross of Christ and His Easter victory are
our hope—our only hope—of real and total liberty
from sin.

Yet for some Christians, in practice, the cross has
become the sign not of the victory of Christ, but of
the victory of the Law. They look upon the cross
chiefly as the sign of that punishment which is due to
all who violate the Law. Such punishment was not
due to Christ, they reason, but He took it upon Himself anyway, because of the great reverence due to the
Law, and to show us how terrible a thing it is to
break it.

Hence, in a strange, unconscious misunderstanding
of the cross, we begin to act as if the cross were the
greatest, most inescapable vindication of the Law. It
is as if for us the blood of Christ had been shed not to
deliver us from the Law by fulfilling it perfectly, once
for all, in Himself. It is rather as if the blood of the
Redeemer had been poured out in order to satiate
and strengthen the Law forever, so that it could never
die but would live on with the eternal sanction of a
just God.

Both these aberrations are terrible in their falsity.
Christ died on the cross, fulfilling the Law and thus
becoming, for all those who are united to Him by
loving faith, their complete fulfillment of the Law.
"So, there is now no longer any condemnation against

those who are in Christ Jesus. The norm of action of the spiritually minded which directs my life in Christ Jesus has delivered me from the inclination that entices me to sin and leads to death" (Rom. 8:2–2).

Nevertheless the Law remains the potential judge and adversary of each one of us, and it regains its grip on us as soon as we begin once more to live "according to the flesh," whether we do so by actual sin, or whether we merely substitute a fleshly and formalistic life of worship for the true eucharistic life in Christ.

The tenacious survival of the Law is no accident. It is intended by God, that the battle of Christ against the Law might continue in mankind until the end of time. It is necessary that this battle continue, and it continues in our own lives.

Why do we secretly keep cherishing a spirituality that is based on the Law rather than on Christ? Why do we fall back into dread, and fail to trust? Because it takes greater courage, more virile energy and more complete sacrifice of ourselves to embrace the liberty of Christ than to remain under slavery to the Law.

We can always evade this issue by confusing liberty with license and saying that in practice the two are indistinguishable. So that, according to this convenient theory, if one does not cling to the Law he will fall into license. There is no such thing for us as St Augustine's "Love and do what you will!" We cannot call Augustine a heretic, of course, but we would certainly like to condemn this statement of his, and most of us seldom hesitate to do so with all the force of our outraged righteousness. Is this perhaps because we have a false notion of Christian liberty? Let us remember St Anselm's doctrine that the "power to sin" is in fact not a power and has nothing to do with the true nature of freedom. He who is truly free is the one who has abandoned sin and renounced it so that, by God's grace, he is no longer inclined to choose evil.

We conveniently forget the real meaning of Augustine's aphorism. One who loves God, one for whom the love of God has replaced the "Law" as the guiding force of his life, does not want anything that is contrary to God's love. The moment he wilfully abandons the way of love and turns aside to will what is contrary to love, he loses his liberty, and falls once again under the tyranny of the Law.

And there, of course, he no longer can "do what he wills," he has to do what the Law prescribes, or else fall further under the deadly tyranny of sin. And the wages of sin is death.

Is the liberty of Christ then a scandal? Yes, frankly it is. It is too much for us, because we do not seriously consider plunging into a life of great apparent risks in order that we may be supported by the hidden power of God and guided by the Holy Spirit.

Indeed, this kind of thing has been viewed with the utmost suspicion. The risks are very real. Have there not been heresies that appealed presumptuously to grace? Have there not been great sinners who combined false mysticism with unbridled license under the pretext that they could love and do what they willed?

There have. But if we think that this is a reason for abandoning the liberty of the sons of God and putting ourselves once more under the Law, *we have emptied the Easter mystery of its most serious implications for our Christian life.*

Let us not therefore make the mistake of thinking that Christian perfection means binding ourselves tighter and tighter in a net of stricter and more minute prescriptions. The great sacrifices of the saints, their mortifications and their penances, so often misleading and misunderstood, were dictated not by Law but by the "spirit of life in Christ Jesus who had delivered them from the law of death" and their Christian greatness consists precisely in the fact that these acts were free, spontaneous and beyond any demand of Law.

It is for this reason that what is good for one saint is not good for another. What is a manifestation of liberty in one might be a sign of slavery in another. Those who consecrate themselves to God in the state of perfection should avoid all servile imitation of others in works that are of counsel, and which should proceed from our own spontaneous gift. The practices of others must never become for us a kind of law which we are bound to try to observe in fear. This is the secret of the shipwreck of many vocations.

Realization of this truth was perhaps what inspired some of the saints, like Francis of Assisi or Philip Neri, with acts of "holy folly" which remind us of the *yurodivetsvo,* the "folly for Christ," familiar in the spirituality of the Russian Church.

Those who keep the commandments of God in a spirit of servile fear, and thus make themselves "slaves of the Law," are often unconsciously striving to use the Law as cloak for the evil they feel in themselves. They try to observe the Law in such a way that the evil they do may not be imputed to them. And in this they subtly endeavor to turn the Law inside out, so that it becomes not their accuser but their defender.

But they cannot do this without tampering with the letter, stretching and distorting the meaning of the Law to make it cover their particular "cases." They do not realize that this manipulation of the letter turns the Law into a most deadly instrument. It is above all the legal-minded that "the letter killeth" at the very instant when they believe themselves to be saved by it.

Even when we are most sincere in our subjection to the Law, it remains a tyranny which is not willed for us by Christ, a tyranny from which He died to deliver us. Once again, let us turn to St Paul and try to grasp the real meaning of our Christian liberty.

The most important thing that strikes us when we read the Pauline Epistles objectively, is that most of the things that many sincerely pious Christians worry about are things which do not matter:

Let no one then call you to account for what you eat or drink, or for the observance of a festival or a new moon or a sabbath. These are but shadows of the realities which were to come, but the reality is Christ. . . . If you have died with Christ to the rudimentary notions which the world has to offer, why do you act as though you still belonged to the world by submitting to such rules as "Do not touch; do not taste; do not handle"! These are formulated according to merely human precepts and doctrines about things that perish in their very use. To be sure these rules have a show of wisdom with their self-imposed worship, their practices of humiliation and their unspar-ing treatment of the body, *but they are not to be held in esteem since they lead to the gratification of our lower nature.* (Col. 2:16–18, 20–23).

We must face the fact that the challenge of a pas-sage like this is too much for many pious Christians. It is much too hot to handle. But if we are risen with Christ, if we are not "enemies of the cross of Christ," and if we believe in Christ's victory over the Law, we are going to have to understand works like these and put them into practice in our lives.

What is the trouble? Once again, it is this. We look at the Law as *the only possible alternative to sin.* There is the flesh, and there is the Law. Either you keep the Law, or the flesh carries you away. One or the other. It is better to keep the Law. Slavery to the Law is less degrading, less humiliating, and indeed it almost seems to endow us with a certain dignity. We are servants not just of the Law, but of God the Law-giver. Unfortunately the cross and resurrection of Christ are there to make this evasion inexcusable.

If we look carefully at the famous contrast made by St Paul between the "law of God in his mind" and "the law of sin in his body" we will see a little more in it than just these two.

It is true, St Paul says he is "delighted with God's law according to the inner man," with his "mind he serves the law of God but with his lower nature the law which allures him to sin" (Rom. 7:22, 24, 25). Ordinarily this text is not interpreted fully. Very often for instance we take it to mean that there is nothing else for us but to accept this inevitable con-flict, to try to keep the law of God in spite of the bias of concupiscence that draws us toward sin. To accept the conflict in a spirit of Christian resignation is all that is required of us as Christians.

Do we not see that this leaves us purely and simply captives of the Law? If this is all there is to it, then Christ's victory is not complete in our lives.

There is a third possibility, and this is the right one. It is the grace of God in Christ our Lord or, to be more succinct, *it is Christ Himself in us.* It is our new life in Christ. By our life of love and hope in Christ we rise above the dilemma and thus resolve it.

The Christian solution is not merely to continue struggling against temptation in order to live according to the Law. This is nothing new. It is exactly what had to be done before the coming of Christ. The Christian is no longer bound by the law of the flesh, and he is no longer obliged in a spirit of fear to keep the Law of God considered as a formal code imposed on him from without.

He may still be tempted by the flesh. He resists temptation and is saved not by various practices and stratagems but *by the spiritual force of love itself, and of the new life that is in him.* He lives by the "Spirit of him who raised Christ Jesus from the dead," and by that Spirit he "puts to death the deeds prompted by the animal instincts, and so lives" (Rom. 8:11, 13).

In other words, it is not dutiful observance that keeps us from sin, but something far greater: it is love. And this love is not something which we develop by our own powers alone. It is a sublime gift of the divine mercy, and the fact that we live in the realization of this mercy and this gift is the greatest source of growth for our love and for our holiness.

This gift, this mercy, this unbounded love of God for us has been lavished upon us as a result of Christ's victory. To taste this love is to share in His victory. To realize our freedom, to exult in our liberation from death, from sin and from the Law, is to sing the *Alleluia* which truly glorifies God in this world and in the world to come.

This joy in God, this freedom which raises us in faith and in hope above the bitter struggle that is the lot of man caught between the flesh and the Law, this is the new canticle in which we join with the blessed angels and the saints in praising God.

God who is rich in mercy, was moved by the intense love with which he loved us, and when we were dead by reason of our transgressions, he made us live with the life of Christ . . . Together with Christ Jesus and in him he raised us up and enthroned us in the heavenly realm . . . It is by grace that you have been saved through faith; it is the gift of God, it is not the result of anything you did, so that no one has any grounds for boasting.

(Eph. 2:4–9)

Let us not then darken the joy of Christ's victory by remaining in captivity and in darkness, but let us declare His power, by living as free men who have been called by Him out of darkness into his admirable light.

[1959]

II

THE GOOD SAMARITAN

"Who is my neighbor?"
Christ told the parable of the Good Samaritan in answer to that question.

To us, all Samaritans are "Good Samaritans." But it was not so to those who first heard the parable. In their eyes all Samaritans were, by the very fact, bad. Indeed that was why a Samaritan had to be the subject of the parable. It was necessary for the hearers to realize that at least one Samaritan could be a good one.

We on the other hand accept Samaritans without difficulty as good, having identified ourselves with them. All Samaritans are good in our eyes because we consider ourselves Samaritans—and good ones. Since we have come to regard ourselves as good Samaritans, do we not perhaps consider that Jews are less good than ourselves? In that case we will not understand the parable at all, for we shall imagine that the priest and Levite passes by the wounded man just because they were Jews. And we shall think that it was because the Samaritan was both "good" and "samaritan" that he helped him.

But if we interpret the parable in this way we close our minds to its meaning. For neither the Jew nor the Samaritan is our neighbor in any exclusive or comforting sense.

Consider the question that was asked: "Who is my neighbor?" This was, in fact, the second of two questions which a lawyer asked of Christ. His first, intended as a temptation or an embarrassment, was, "How shall I obtain eternal life?" This is an important question, and so important that nobody can be without the answer to it. And note that he asks this question of Him of Whom we read: "This is eternal life: to know Thee, the One True God, and Jesus Christ Whom Thou hast sent."

Since the answer to the most important of questions is accessible to everyone, the lawyer should have known it. And he did know it. He had no need to ask it at all. The Lord made this clear, for He said: "What is the first commandment?" When the lawyer replied, saying that the first commandment was the love of God and of our neighbor, then Christ told him to keep that commandment and he would have eternal life. In this way it became clear that the question was not necessary. But in order to prove that he had not asked it without reason the lawyer asked another question: "Who is my neighbor?"

We can perhaps assume that he meant by this to suggest that he had no problem about loving God, since "God is good," but that he was perplexed about loving his neighbor, since some men are better than others, and all are imperfect. This being the case, in order to protect himself against loving an unworthy object and thus wasting his love, he wanted to know where to draw the line. Who is the neighbor to be loved, who is the alien not to be loved? The question is a matter of rational classification. Therefore it is a matter of judgement also, for to classify is to judge. How then does one classify people, and judge them accurately as worthy of love, or of hatred, or of indifference? This is a pretty problem. But to the Lord it was a problem that had no meaning, for He said, "Judge not, that ye be not judged." Do not classify, and do not be classified.

The parable seems not to answer this question, or at least not to answer it directly. For the lawyer is saying, "How shall I identify my neighbor, in order actively to *give* him the love that is commanded by God?" and Christ gives an example of one who *needs* love, and who passively *receives* love from someone who falls outside the category of "neighbor." And yet the Samaritan is constituted a "neighbor" by the fact that he gives love. Now what this answer really says is more than the scribe explicitly asked. For the answer cuts right through the question.

Christ does not tell the scribe how to judge and classify, but teaches him that classifications are without significance in this matter of love. For we do not and cannot love according to classifications. Or if we do, then we do not love in the full sense of the word. Love is free, and does not need a good object: it can confer goodness that is hidden. But if love submits itself to an object, to a good outside itself, it tends to its own destruction. If it confers good upon its object, then it thrives and grows. For the nature of love is to give as well as to receive. It both gives and receives, but it gives first, and in giving it receives. Therefore if love demands first of all to receive a good from its object, before beginning to love, then it can never begin to love.

If a man has to be pleasing to me, comforting, reassuring, before I can love him, then I cannot truly love him. Not that love cannot console or reassure! But if I demand *first* to be reassured, I will never dare to begin loving. If a man has to be a Jew or a Christian before I can love him, then I cannot love him. If he has to be black or white before I can love him, then I cannot love him. If he has to belong to my political party or social group before I can love him, if he has to wear my kind of uniform, then my love is no longer love because it is not free: it is dictated by something outside itself. It is dominated by an appetite other than love. I love not the person but his classification, and in that event I love him not as a person but as a thing. I love his label which confirms me in attachment to my own label. But in that case I do not even love myself. I value myself not for what I am, but for my label, my classification. In this way I remain at the mercy of forces outside myself, and those who seem to me to be neighbors are indeed strangers for I am first of all a stranger to myself.

Do you think perhaps this is the meaning of the parable: that all men are to be loved because they are men? Because they are human, and have the same nature? No, this is not the meaning. That would be simply a matter of extending the classification to its broadest limits, and including all men in one big category, "Man." Christ however means more than this, for he gives a more than philosophical answer. His answer is a divine revelation, not a natural ethical principle. It is a revelation of the mystery of God. Hence in revealing truth, it remains mysterious and in some sense hidden. Yet if we get as close as we can to the source of revelation, we can gain deeper insight into the mystery.

The parable of the Good Samaritan is a revelation of God in a word that has great importance through all the Scriptures from the beginning to the end. It is a revelation of what the prophet Hosea says, speaking for the invisible God, "I will have *mercy* and not sacrifices." What is this *mercy* which we find spoken of everywhere in the Scriptures, and especially in the Psalms? The Vulgate rings with *misericordia* as though with a deep church bell. Mercy is the "burden" or the "bourdon," it is the bass bell and undersong of the whole Bible. But the Hebrew word which we render as mercy, *misericordia,* says more still than mercy.

Chesed (mercy) is also fidelity, it is also strength. It is the faithful, the indefectible mercy of God. It is ultimate and unfailing because it is the power that binds one person to another, in a covenant of wills. It is the power that binds us to God because He has promised us mercy and will never fail in His promise. For He cannot fail. It is the power and the mercy which are most characteristic of Him, which come nearer to the mystery into which we enter when all concepts darken and evade us.

There are other attributes of God which are further from Him and nearer to ourselves. They come and go in the Scriptures. They are flashes and presences, they appear and disappear as if they were in some sense provisional, as if they were approximations: they are too partial! All concepts of God have to be corrected and completed in so far as they are analogies. Some however more than others. For example the metaphor that He is angry, when in fact He is not angry. It is true that He manifests His wrath, that He judges, He punishes and He "strikes"! But when we say that He does all these things, He does not do them but something else which we do not understand. And when it has been said that He is angry it has only been said that it seemed to us that He was angry. We are saying that if *we* had been in His place we would have been angry and would have struck. But because "my thoughts are not your thoughts, says the Lord," there is something much nearer the truth which appears on a transcendent level when the anger vanishes. This is the sun which does not change, behind the passing clouds which are other attributes of God. This unchanging, fundamental, stable element is the mystery which is revealed in the Hebrew word *chesed*.

What do we read in Isaiah?

For the Lord hath called thee as a woman forsaken and mourning in spirit, and as a wife cast off from her youth, said thy God. For a small moment have I forsaken thee, but with great mercies will I gather thee.

In a moment of indignation have I hid my face a

little from thee, but with everlasting kindness have I
had mercy on thee, said the Lord thy Redeemer.

(Isa. 54:6–8)

Again Hosea says that the Lord does not want to be
called Lord so much as "husband," since to be called
Lord is to be worshipped with fear rather than love,
as though He were a Baal and not a Savior. For it is
characteristic of a Baal to have no *chesed*. The power
of the Baal is another power, frightening and capri-
cious, but unable to reach the depths of our own
being. *Chesed* can take possession of our hearts and
transform them and so it is said

And it shall be in that day, saith the Lord, That she
shall call me: My husband, and she shall call me no
more Baal.
And I will take away the names of Baalim out of her
mouth, and she shall no more remember their name.

(Hosea 2:16–17)

Again *chesed* is something more than mercy. But it
contains in itself many varied aspects of God's love
which flash forth in mercy and are its fountain and its
hidden source. Remember how God revealed Himself
to Moses on Sinai. First Moses had begged to see His
face, and the Lord had told Moses that no one could
see Him and live. Moses had pleaded to see Him, so
God showed Himself without showing Himself. That
is to say that Moses saw Him by not seeing Him, since
he saw Him when He was gone. But He "had been"
there (He who is everywhere and nowhere). That is
to say that Moses having first known Him in complete
darkness without seeing Him, then saw Him in a

kind of light-after-darkness without knowing Him. First the dark flash and the passing and the night, then the cries and words drawn out of the depths of the darkness and mystery of that awakening. These great words shot up out of the heart of Moses and exploded in various shapes and tones which all formed the figure of *chesed:*

> O the Lord, the Lord God, merciful and gracious, patient and of much compassion and true, who keepest mercy unto thousands: who takest away iniquity and wickedness and sin, and no man of himself is innocent before thee.

> (Exodus 34:6–7)

The *chesed* of God is a gratuitous mercy that considers no fitness, no worthiness and no return. It is the way the Lord looks upon the guilty and with His look makes them at once innocent. This look seems to some to be anger because they fly from it. But if they face it they see that it is love and that they are innocent. (Their flight and the confusion of their own fear make them guilty in their own eyes.) The *chesed* of God is truth. It is infallible strength. It is the love by which He seeks and chooses His chosen, and binds them to Himself. It is the love by which He is married to mankind, so that if humanity is faithless to Him it must still always have a fidelity to which to return: that is His own fidelity. He has become inseparable from man in the *chesed* which we call "Incarnation," and "Cross," and "Resurrection." He has also given us His *chesed* in the Person of His Spirit. The Paraclete is the full, inexpressible mystery of *chesed.* So that in the depths of our own being there is an inexhaustible spring of mercy and of love. Our own being has become love. Our own self has become God's love for us, and it is full of Christ, of *chesed*. But we must face it and accept it. We must accept ourselves and others as *chesed*. We must be to ourselves and to others signs and sacraments of mercy.

Chesed, mercy and power, manifests itself visibly in the *chasid*, or the saint. Indeed the saint is one whose whole life is immersed in the *chesed* of God. The saint is the instrument of the divine mercy. Through the *chasid* the love of God reaches into the world in a visible mystery, a mystery of poverty and love, meekness and power. The *chasid* is in many respects a foolish one, who has been made comical by mercy. For the apparent tragedy of his nothingness is turned inside out with joy. In his folly the divine wisdom shines forth and his annihilation is a new creation, so that he rejoices in the incongruity of the divine mercies and is everlastingly astonished at the creative love of God. He calls upon all beings to praise this love with him, and most of them do not pay attention. Yet the sun and moon and the sea and the hills and stars join him, nevertheless, in praising *chesed*. The majority of men, perhaps, consider him crazy.

(God, too, is glad to be thought crazy in His *chasid*. For the wisdom of God is folly in the eyes of men.)

The folly of the *chasid* is manifested in his love and concern for his neighbor, the sinner. For the sinner is "next to" the *chasid* or the saint. They are so close to one another, so like one another, that they are sometimes almost indistinguishable. The professionally pious man, on the contrary, makes a whole career out of being distinguishable from sinners. He wants it to

be very clear to God and to man that he and the
sinner are in different categories. Hence the love of
the *chasid* for the sinner (and of the sinner for the
chasid) is not the patronizing concern of the pious
and respectable, but the impractical concern of one
who acts as if he thought he were the sinner's mother
and brother and sister. Such a one behaves like the
Samaritan in the parable, and not like the priest and
Levite, who were well aware of proprieties, and classifications, and categories. Who knows? Perhaps the
priest took a look at the character lying in the ditch
and observed that he had blood all over him and that
it would never do to contract a ritual impurity. Especially out here in the desert, miles from water. Those
who are professionally respectable, and whose lives
are measured out in long and formal ceremonies,
have other things to do than to be instruments of
chesed.

Who, then, is my neighbor? To whom am I bound?
Whom must I love?

These are not intelligent questions, and they do
not have clear answers. On the contrary any attempt
to answer them involves us in endless subtleties, and
vagueness, and ultimate confusion. Love knows no
classifications. The measure of love that Christ has set
for us is beyond measure: we must "be perfect as the
heavenly Father is perfect." But what is meant by the
"perfection" of the heavenly Father? It is imparti-
ality, not in the sense of justice that measures out
equally to all, knowing their merits, but in the sense
of *chesed* that knows no classification of good and
evil, just or unjust. "For He sends His rain upon the
just and the unjust."

We are bound to God in *chesed*. The power of His mercy has taken hold of us and will not let go of us: therefore we have become foolish. We can no longer love wisely. And because we have emptied ourselves in this folly which He has sent upon us, we can be moved by His unpredictable wisdom, so that we love whom we love and we help whom we help, not according to plans of our own but according to the measure laid down for us in His hidden will, which knows no measure. In this folly, which is the work of His Spirit, we must love especially those who are helpless and who can do nothing for themselves. We must also receive love from them, realizing our own helplessness, and our own inability to fend for ourselves. *Chesed* had made us as though we were outcasts and sinners. *Chesed* has numbered us among the aliens and strangers: *chesed* has not only robbed us of our reason but declassified us along with everyone else, in the sight of God. Thus we have no home, no family, no niche in society, and no recognizable function. Nor do we even appear to be especially charitable, and we cannot pride ourselves on virtue. *Chesed* had apparently robbed us of all that, for he who lives by the mercy of God alone shall have nothing else to live by, only that mercy. *Plenitudo legis est charitas.* Mercy fulfills the whole law.

The mystery of the Good Samaritan is this, then: the mystery of *chesed*, power and mercy. In the end, it is Christ Himself who lies wounded by the roadside. It is Christ Who comes by in the person of the Samaritan. And Christ is the bond, the compassion and the understanding between them. This is how the Church is made of living stones, compacted together

in mercy. Where there is on the one hand a helpless
one, beaten and half dead, and on the other an out-
cast with no moral standing and the one leans down
in pity to help the other, then there takes place
a divine epiphany and awakening. There is "man,"
there reality is made human, and in answer to this
movement of compassion a Presence is made on the
earth, and the bright cloud of the majesty of God
overshadows their poverty and their love. There may
be no consolation in it. There may be nothing humanly charming about it. It is not necessarily like the
movies. Perhaps the encounter is outwardly sordid
and unattractive. But the Presence of God is brought
about on earth there, and Christ is there, and God is
in communion with man.

This is what we are talking about when we speak of
"doing the will of God." Not only fulfilling precepts,
and praying, and being holy, but being instruments
of mercy, and fastening ourselves and others to God
in the bonds of *chesed.*

The two questions asked by the scribe were, then,
useless. Therefore Christ did not answer them. Yet
He did not pass them by without attention. On the
contrary, He saw them as indications of the scribe's
plight and of our own. Instead of answering the
question, He poured oil and wine into the wounds.
This He did by His own words, Who is Himself the
answer to all useful questions.

[1961]